Praise for *Rare Leadership*

Leaders who are unloving and unaware of the importance of relationships can do a great deal of harm—I have seen it. I commend Dr. Wilder and Dr. Warner for their innovative and deeply compassionate approach to helping leaders become more loving, more mature, and more effective.

—**GARY CHAPMAN**, PhD, bestselling author, *The 5 Love Languages*®

There are simple, common reasons leaders burn out or blow up—or simply lose their joy. I am a leader; I've counseled many leaders. This book rings so true, and *hopeful*, because it offers immensely wise and practical help, together with enough illustrations to show us the way.

—**JOHN ELDREDGE**, author of *Wild at Heart* and *Moving Mountains*, president of Ransomed Heart Ministries

It's rare to find a book that links "joy," modern brain science, and biblical wisdom as a model for leadership. *Rare Leadership* not only does that well—it succeeds in giving leaders four habits that can't help but unleash joy and greater effectiveness and authenticity and endurance in their relationships with others. You'll come away from reading this book knowing much more about how we are "fearfully and wonderfully" made—and far better equipped to lead and love the way Jesus did.

—**JOHN TRENT**, PhD, author of *The Blessing* and *LifeMapping*, Gary D. Chapman Chair of Marriage and Family Ministry and Therapy, Moody Theological Seminary

Regardless of how many leadership books you have read, *Rare Leadership* provides refreshing, challenging and practical lessons for developing leaders (and becoming one) that I will be using for myself and my team.

—**PAUL WHITE**, PhD, psychologist, coauthor, *The 5 Languages of Appreciation at Work*, *Rising Above a Toxic Workplace*, and *Sync or Swim*

I love it. I love it when I don't have to work through the fluff and fight the smog to get to the essentials in a book. *Rare Leadership* by Marcus Warner and Jim Wilder is just that—rare. The content is fresh. The presentation is crisp. The concepts are portable. The results will be obvious.

—SAM CHAND, leadership consultant and author of *Leadership Pain*

Rare Leadership deserves its place with the great leadership books of our time. What *Good to Great* did for organizations, *Rare Leadership* does for individual leaders. It provides the research-based science driving the real-world disciplines and practices of exceptional leaders. While John Maxwell gave us laws for leadership, Wilder and Warner have provided the tools to retrain our brains and grow our hearts into the leaders that our teams will want to follow.

—DAWN WHITESTONE, MA, LMHC, president of Relational Wealth Builders

This book provides a process driven approach to loving others well through leadership. Instead of just another list of leadership to-dos or no-no's, this book combines reasoned, accessible brain science and sound Christ-centered relationship principles to provide a valuable roadmap ahead for those willing to apply its truths.

—MATTHEW TURVEY, PsyD, associate director, WinShape Marriage

Healthy leadership is rare leadership in most organizations. And yet the search continues as people around the world look for the secret ingredients to become centered, effective, and transformational leaders. Marcus Warner and Jim Wilder's take the reader to the destination they desire. Their insightful research touches an inflection point that the RARE leadership we seek comes from within and to achieve this we just need to change our mindset.

—ROBERT DICKIE III, president, Crown, author of *The Leap*

Rare Leadership uniquely captures what it takes to be an authentic leader with immeasurable impact, by bringing transformational truths to the marketplace. If you desire to be a leader who ignites transformation this book is a profoundly relevant and timely resource for our generation.

—TINA DYER, vice president of a Fortune 500 company,
    leadership and professional development consultant

Marcus Warner / Jim Wilder

Rare
Leadership

4 Uncommon Habits for Increasing Trust, Joy,
and Engagement in the People You Lead

MOODY PUBLISHERS

CHICAGO

All Scripture quotations, unless otherwise indicated, are taken from the Holy Bible, New International Version`, NIV`. Copyright © 1973, 1978, 1984, 2011 by Biblica, Inc.™ Used by permission of Zondervan. All rights reserved worldwide. www.zondervan.com. The "NIV" and "New International Version" are trademarks registered in the United States Patent and Trademark Office by Biblica, Inc.™

Scripture quotations marked KJV are taken from the King James Version.

Scripture quotations marked ESV are from The Holy Bible, English Standard Version® (ESV®), copyright © 2001 by Crossway, a publishing ministry of Good News Publishers. Used by permission. All rights reserved.

Edited by Elizabeth Cody Newenhuyse
Cover design: Gilbert & Carlson Design LLC dba Gearbox
Cover image of trees copyright © by ykononova/Shutterstock (254219002). All rights reserved.
Jim Wilder photo: Christopher Kamman
Interior design: Erik M. Peterson

Library of Congress Cataloging-in-Publication Data

Names: Warner, Marcus, author. | Wilder, E. James, 1952- author.
Title: Rare leadership : 4 uncommon habits for increasing trust, joy, and
    engagement in the people you lead / Marcus Warner, E. James Wilder.
Description: Chicago : Moody Publishers, 2016. | Includes bibliographical
    references.
Identifiers: LCCN 2016001936 (print) | LCCN 2016002629 (ebook) | ISBN
9780802414540 | ISBN 9780802494436 ()
Subjects: LCSH: Leadership--Religious aspects--Christianity. | Leadership.
Classification: LCC BV4597.53.L43 W37 2016 (print) | LCC BV4597.53.L43
(ebook) | DDC 253--dc23
LC record available at http://lccn.loc.gov/2016001936

We hope you enjoy this book from Moody Publishers. Our goal is to provide high-quality, thought-provoking books and products that connect truth to your real needs and challenges. For more information on other books and products written and produced from a biblical perspective, go to www.moodypublishers.com or write to:

Moody Publishers
820 N. La Salle Boulevard
Chicago, IL 60610

3 5 7 9 10 8 6 4

Printed in the United States of America

*We dedicate this book to all of our kingdom colleagues
who pour their hearts into ministry.
We hope this book will encourage and guide you
to greater joy in all you do.*

Contents

Foreword

"**HOW MANY OF YOU** have ever worked for a terrible boss?" This is the question I often ask audiences when I start my talks on leadership. How would you respond? I love the topic of leadership because leaders make things happen. Leaders affect all of us, whether we lead, follow, or try to stay out of the way. History is the story of leaders—good and bad ones that have done amazing good and terrible evil. I have a huge passion to help people starting out in leadership get on the right track and not make the awful mistakes that make life miserable for followers.

When I ask that "terrible boss" question, without fail, ninety percent of the audience raises their hands and rolls their eyes. I also get a lot of soft moans. It is like they are saying, "Hans, if only you knew the half of it!"

Why are there so many leaders out there that are really tough to trust and follow? Honestly, I think it has to do with their lack of being emotionally healthy. One of the biggest mistakes people make in the realm of leadership is focusing too much on *"what am I to do?"* as opposed to *"who am I to be?"* Yes, I confess that in my thirty years of leadership—practicing it, writing books about it, and teaching the topic—I have often fallen into that performance trap. And face it—most boards evaluate their leaders based on performance and results.

I so much appreciate this refreshing book you hold in your hands,

Rare Leadership. Dr. Jim Wilder and Dr. Marcus Warner have given us an amazing resource that goes right to the heart of healthy leadership. The thesis of this book is that "rare leadership" is the fruit of four uncommon habits related to emotional intelligence. These are 1) remain relational, 2) act like yourself, 3) return to joy, and 4) endure hardship.

Why is this kind of leadership *rare?* It is rare because it focuses on being a healthy person under the water line. In recent years I have become more convinced than ever that being an effective, healthy leader is more about your EQ than your IQ. It is about who you are, not what you do. The four uncommon habits that Jim Wilder and Marcus Warner describe in this book are groundbreaking in this space of emotional intelligence in leadership.

In case *emotional intelligence* (EQ) is new to you, it is what I call the soft side of leadership. It is all about the kind of person we are underneath the surface, and how we interact with others. It's known as EQ as opposed to IQ, which is our intelligence quotient. Success in leadership has so much more to do with EQ than IQ. We all have seen a lot of really smart people utterly fail as leaders. Through some of my own failures, I've come to believe that emotional intelligence is essential for effective, healthy leadership. The key word there is "healthy."

People don't like to follow dysfunctional leaders. Sometimes they have to, but they don't want to. I could tell you a lot of horror stories I've collected over the years of individuals that have been horrible employers, team leaders, and bosses. Isn't it amazing how many dysfunctional people can become the boss or team leader? Why do they get up there when they are so unhealthy? It could be money, politics, or just the accidental fact that they got there first. What *you* need to focus on is becoming a great, healthy leader as you grow in your influence.

Traditionally, when being evaluated for a job, managers tended to look for the hard skills such as experience, degrees, training, and how well they could perform a task. But according to a ton of new research, performance success in leadership is one-third IQ and two-thirds EQ. Or to put it another way, emotional intelligence counts for twice as much as IQ and technical skills combined to be successful in leading others.

This is not another one of those high-octane type "A" leadership performance books. It is about matters of your heart and the person you are becoming as a healthy leader that people will follow with joy. I highly recommend this book to every leader that wants to make a mark and leave a God-honoring legacy.

Dr. Hans Finzel
Author of *The Top Ten Mistakes Leaders Make*
Highlands Ranch, Colorado
www.hansfinzel.com

Preface

I (MARCUS) wanted to write this book because I needed it so much when I was pastoring, and because I see so many Christian organizations struggling with the same challenges again and again. Most of these leadership challenges have less to do with strategic planning than the ability to handle difficult relationships and upsetting emotions. Once I knew I wanted to write the book, there was no question who I wanted to work with me. It had to be Jim Wilder. Most of what I have learned about the issues taught in this book were ideas and practices I picked up from him.

If you are the sort of leader who just wants the basics as quickly as possible, I suggest you start reading with Part 2—"Building RARE Leadership." If you are the sort who likes to understand the philosophical foundations and paradigms beneath the practices, then read it all.

Too often leaders are chosen simply on gifting, education, and experience. We give lip service to the idea of maturity, but do we really know how to assess maturity? More to the point, do we have a clear strategy for helping people grow maturity? Giving them good information and holding them accountable for their choices is not enough. There is so much more that needs to be woven into the fabric of Christian organizations.

We hope this book challenges you. Even more, we hope it sets out a clear path to how people grow and how you can experience both personal and corporate transformation.

Introduction

YOU'VE PROBABLY HEARD the term "emotional intelligence," or EQ. If you're familiar with the concept, you know that emotional intelligence can make you a better leader and help you build a healthy organization. But did you also know that people with a high degree of emotional intelligence earn an average of $29,000 more per year than people with a low degree of emotional intelligence?[1] I would extrapolate from this data that they earn this premium because they do significantly more than their peers to realize their organization's mission.

But whether you're leading a multimillion-dollar corporation or launching a new church plant, you can benefit from this book and the profound insights shared by Dr. Jim Wilder and Dr. Marcus Warner. The thesis of this book is that the fruit of four uncommon habits related to emotional intelligence is a *dramatic increase in trust, joy, and engagement in the people you lead.*

Perhaps the term "aha moment" is overused. Yet I suspect you also have those books that have completely changed the way you've approached your life, your work, and your leadership. Among that very short list of real game-changers for me are:

The Seven Habits of Highly Effective People
Getting Things Done
The Power of Full Engagement

There were nuggets I took from each of these books that really changed the way I saw things.

Along with these game-changing books, I've had the privilege of knowing Jim Wilder for over twenty-five years. Jim codeveloped the groundbreaking "Life Model" whose principles inspired this book. He is the coauthor of the book *Living from the Heart Jesus Gave You*, which has sold over 100,000 copies and been translated into eleven languages. He has taught leaders all around the world to spread joy through relational skills. And his work has changed my life and leadership.

The four uncommon habits that he and Dr. Marcus Warner describe in this book have also had a tremendous impact on my family, my career, and the teams I have been privileged to lead. Here, Dr. Wilder and Dr. Warner combine experience working with leaders and churches, biblical insights, and the latest brain science research to explore what it means to be a RARE leader. Briefly, here's what that means:

REMAIN RELATIONAL

I began my career as a very task-oriented individual. It was easy for me to sell to accountants and attorneys who were also very task-oriented. It was harder for me to sell to highly relational people. I had to learn how to tell stories. I still remember practicing a story about something that happened to me on a golf course so that I could tell it as needed during a sales call. The idea that *the relationship is more important than the problem* took a long time for me to believe, and I still haven't mastered it. If you are like me, you've been rewarded for being a problem solver. Knocking down the barriers to get results comes easily to you. But figuring out how to develop a deep and lasting culture that furthers and deepens your organization's mission while building its capacity is a challenge. For some of us, it is almost a foreign language.

But here I am reminded of something Stephen Covey talks about that I have never forgotten: the idea of production capacity versus production. You can focus on production at the expense of capacity and get stellar short-term results. But long-term results will always require investing in capacity. If relationships are the root of joy, and joy is the jet fuel of high-performing teams, it follows that learning to remain relational is a key factor in creating high-performing teams and building healthy churches and organizations.

ACT LIKE YOURSELF

Have you ever seen a display of uncontrolled anger improve the performance of a team? I've never seen that. I have seen uncontrolled anger destroy an organization.

I grew up prone to anger. I'm an excitable extrovert, proud of my Italian heritage, which many link with effusiveness—including effusiveness with anger. Years ago Jim Wilder taught me this idea of "acting like myself." It was part of a series of questions he suggested I ask myself when faced with a strong, unpleasant emotion. What is it like me and my people to do when I feel a certain emotion? In other words, *What would the person God made me to be do? What would Jesus do? What would the people of God functioning at their best do?* Jim gives the example of Jesus becoming so angry one time that He healed someone. One thing I learned that always stuck with me was that it is like my best self to protect others from my anger.

I've been in many situations where this inability of a leader to act like "his best self" has led to a downward spiral in morale, resulting in the loss of very capable employees. Each of these leaders had a long list of fine qualities. They might be charming and fun to be around, able to recruit very qualified talent and highly intelligent. Yet each one experienced those moments when something would set them off. One might experience a surge of anger, which would completely eclipse his ability to remain his usual charming, fun, relational self. In these moments he would fail to protect others from his anger. Some fired talented team members in outbursts of rage. Others rattled team members to the point that they lost their ability to perform (a phenomenon well documented in *Multipliers: How the Best Leaders Make Everyone Smarter*). Other leaders' occasional tirades created such a climate of fear and anxiety that some employees lost all desire to perform.

RETURN TO JOY

The idea that joy is the ultimate jet fuel, the purest and most potent source of motivation, is a realization that unleashes tremendous potential in you and your team. Think about yourself for a moment. How productive are you when you are stuck in one of the six unpleasant emotions hardwired into our brains: fear, anger, disgust, shame, sadness, hopelessness? High-performing athletes succeed because they have a quick recovery time. The same is true in leadership. A well-trained brain can return to joy in ninety seconds. A less well-trained brain can take hours, days, even weeks. What is the toll in creativity and productivity of all the lost time while you or those you lead remain stuck in one or more of what we call these "big six" emotions? (See page 209 for a quick guide to RARE terms and concepts.)

ENDURE HARDSHIP

In some ways this may at first seem like one of the easiest lessons for high achievers—or church leaders schooled in the biblical language of struggle and sacrifice. We all know the phrase "no pain, no gain." But this idea of enduring suffering is deeper than that. Jim Wilder often calls it learning to suffer well. We are going to suffer. Our Master suffered. *How do we learn to stay relational and continue to act like ourselves, like the person God made us to be, during suffering?* If we don't learn how to do this we will avoid suffering or spread our suffering to our team. In some ways this might include being "the bigger person." The narcissist leader says, "If anyone is going to suffer, it's not going to be me," and turns the suffering onto the team. The RARE leader says, "If anyone is going to suffer, can it be me? I'm good at it. I know how to do it. I can model it to the team." And this RARE leader can walk with team members in their suffering.

My wish for you is that you will find in these pages those "aha" moments that make you say, "Yes, this makes so much sense. Somehow I knew this was true, but just couldn't put my finger on it."

I pray that you will develop these four uncommon habits and that they will be a blessing to you, your family, and your organization for generations to come.

JIM MARTINI
CEO of Life Model Works

CHAPTER 1

Leadership at the Speed of Joy

Wisdom from the Bible, discoveries from brain science

IF YOU ARE a student of leadership, you know about the importance of engagement and emotional intelligence. You have also read a wide variety of case studies that tell us what successful leaders do. What you probably don't know is that recent developments in brain science now reveal that leadership skills are learned in a different way and in a different area of the brain than management skills and academic studies. We now know how leaders can train this powerful brain system to produce full engagement in their team and develop a high level of emotional intelligence that keeps them plugged into a renewable, high-octane source of motivation.

In this book, we want to help you in two ways: 1) We want you to understand the fast-track brain mechanism that learns and distributes leadership skills, and 2) we want to help you train the leadership system in your brain using four core habits of effective leaders. These four habits will cause your emotional intelligence to soar. As we saw in the introduction, these habits can be remembered with the word RARE. They are:

Remain Relational
Act Like Yourself
Return to Joy
Endure Hardship Well

Many leaders, business people, pastors, team leaders and influencers never receive any training in leadership. This contributes to mistaking management for leadership. Management is the efficient accomplishment of tasks. Leadership is producing and maintaining full engagement from our group in what matters. The RARE leaders we wish to emulate inspire us because they do this well. Now, we will show you how it is done.

ORGANIZATIONAL SKILLS VS. PEOPLE SKILLS

Dr. Chris Shaw has over thirty years of experience training leaders and pastors across Latin America. With two devotional books to his credit, his daily devotional is read by over 6,000 website visitors a day. Dr. Shaw edits a leadership magazine for both men and women leaders with a subscription of 185,000 readers.

> The term "lead" has come to mean organizational skills rather than people skills.

Chris holds his doctorate in leadership development with a thesis on *A Philosophy of Education for Leadership Formation through Theological Studies* at Fuller Seminary. His master's degree was in Christian formation and discipleship. He began teaching as full-time staff at the Buenos Aires Bible Institute and this position opened international doors to conferences where Dr. Shaw draws crowds of pastors.

We asked Chris for his observations on leadership. Chris immediately observed the problems caused by mistaking management skills for leadership. He says:

> *Leadership has become heavily influenced by managerial models, so that the term "lead" has come to mean organizational skills rather than people skills.*

What Chris did not learn in his doctorate program (that we now know) is how leadership skills are learned. The brain uses a "fast-track" process for relational leadership skills and a very different "slow-track" process for management skills. The "fast track" operates at speeds above the level of conscious thought and primarily governs relational reality. The "slow track" is what we notice consciously. It monitors results and provides explanations and solutions to problems we face. (These are challenging concepts, we know. We will explain these ideas more fully at the end of this chapter.[1] For now, understand that both learning processes are super-important.)

But the how is less important than the what—the impact on our organizations and on real people. Chris sees the impact on both pastors and churches. He says:

> *The Kingdom, however, is not about organizations, projects or even ministries. It's about people, and so leadership, in Kingdom terms, would refer to the development of the kind of "people skills" that would help those we have been invited to walk with to achieve their full potential in Christ. This is rare in many church leaders today. Despite the fact that the Church is all about people, I find that many pastors have woefully inadequate people skills, and are often even uncomfortable around others, unless it is within the context of a programmed meeting. Leadership, for many pastors, is exercised from a platform whilst holding onto a microphone.*

Dr. Shaw began his journey by becoming an assistant pastor to a church that was actively planting congregations in the slums of Buenos Aires. In this context he began training young leaders—a practice he continues to this day. He began to notice very quickly that lectures, classes, and Bible studies were needed, but that something was missing.

> *Early on in my pastoral experience I discovered how easy it was to experience painful loneliness whilst being surrounded by a community of believers. The loneliness seemed to point to the fact that many of the congregations that we would describe as communities of faith were really just gatherings of people who happened to meet in the same building at regular times throughout the*

week. Multiple encounters with Christians who felt used (and sometimes discarded) by their leaders moved me to find another leadership model. There was no real interest in them as individuals, aside from the way they fit into or furthered the leader's personal projects. As a resident chaplain at the Bible Institute, I counseled dozens of disenchanted Christians, and it strengthened my resolve to explore alternative leadership training methods.

I was disappointed as a student (and later as a member of faculty) to notice how uninterested many professors were in the lives of their students. Some couldn't even be bothered to learn the names of their students. All their focus seemed to be on getting through their material. When I began to work as part of the faculty I wanted to be a shepherd to my students, and not just somebody who delivered lectures.

Because I speak at a lot of conferences I guess many people would evaluate my success or failure by the number of people I am able to attract to a given event. Perhaps the most frequent phrase I hear, as I travel around Latin America, is how blessed people feel by what I have shared through a presentation, or in my books. My greatest change has been the crystallizing of a concept that I have worked with for many years: "Leaders influence more through who they are than by what they do." Today I place much greater value on the informal moments at an event than the formal times, because they offer me precious opportunities to interact with people on a personal level.

What is that mysterious thing that happens when people interact at a personal level? How does it work? Who taught you leadership, and did you learn how to develop leadership under you for the teams you lead? How can we become more effective? The RARE leaders whose team we would love to join, and whose style we would like to emulate, lead by some means we cannot quite fully capture. We can see they have built a strong repertoire of positive relational habits that produce trust, joy, and engagement around them. Chris could intuitively tell by his own growth that relationship played an important part. (Actually, intuition is another brain process that runs in the fast track. We call it intuition because our mind figures things out *before* we are consciously aware that our brain has been figuring.)

For Chris, his leadership development began when he was invited to join a small, home-based congregation. Chris found great inspiration and encouragement to develop leadership in this relational environment. In time, they founded a leadership magazine, traveled and taught pastors, and even ran a small publishing house. I (Jim) began to travel and teach as part of their international training ministry, too. By then the team was reaching over 60,000 pastors who subscribed to their printed leadership magazine.

Then it happened. The organization was devastated by moral failures. The shakeup that followed left behind distrust, low joy, and a disintegrating ministry for Chris to lead. These are the moments when RARE leadership is required. Chris says,

> *The focus of my work over the next three years became stabilizing the ministry and helping staff to recover from the shock precipitated by this crisis. We began a major process of reorganizing and renewing the focus of the ministry so that it continues to be an effective tool for leadership development in a rapidly changing world.*

How could this leadership failure happen? Two observations will help us at this point. First, the team had all the information, education, and experience needed. They had even heard the Life Model taught and explained multiple times by me, the author. However, all the information had been learned on the slow-track brain system we use for management and not on the fast-track system we use for leadership and guidance.

We have observed that leaders often believe that *understanding* an idea is sufficient to make that idea a reality in their own lives. Many times, our years of success blind us to important flaws. Hidden flaws bring us to our second observation. The common ministry leadership model Chris had learned and distributed through teaching, conferences, counseling advice, and publications gave no importance to joy levels in leaders' lives. Joy is a delight in our relationships with God and others. While faithfulness to God, Scripture, and others seemed important, the loving joy from fellowship and family became an afterthought. Dropping joy levels create risks the way dry conditions affect a forest. Many leadership failures can be traced to declining joy levels in leadership teams, marriages, and families. As joy drops, the "fire danger" reaches critical levels without being noticed. RARE leadership is powered by joy. (We'll explain how to monitor "joy levels" later in the book.[2])

We have found in our study of Scripture and brain science that joy, that feeling of well-being in the deepest part of our soul, is primarily relational. To the human brain, joy is always relational. Even those times of solitude as we dig in our garden or read an absorbing book are relational experiences. More about this later.[3]

We might say that leadership travels at the speed of joy. Joy levels are important in at least three ways.

1. The fast track in the brain is motivated to learn through joy.
2. People with emotional intelligence and relational skills always create joy around them.
3. Leadership skills do not transfer from one person to another in the absence of joy.

Leadership that neglects joy rapidly becomes management instead of leadership. Most people are moved into leadership because they are effective workers. They do more or better work than others. They often do not distinguish improving work productivity from leadership. As leaders manage increasingly larger workloads and focus energy on better productivity, objectives, and results, they easily miss the decline in joy levels in their lives, families, and work teams.

A discussion of how our joy gets low will have to wait until later in this book[4] when we examine the four RARE habits of great leaders more carefully. You can be sure that low joy involves a failed training strategy in how we learn to deal relationally with unpleasant emotions. Chris now says:

The concepts I have learned through The Life Model *have provided some of the answers that I have sought for years. All of the fast-track skills that I have been learning just make so much sense, in light of the priorities that God seems to have been stressing for my own ministry over these past decades. If the Kingdom is all about people, then learning how to stay in relationships, through thick and thin, has got to be something where we excel and that we teach well. The call to leadership for us, then, would seem to be a call to walk with a group of people, as we strive to make our relationship with God visible in the context of the challenges that each day brings our way.*

THE FOUR HABITS OF RARE LEADERS

As we have already seen, the thesis of this book is that there are four uncommon habits developed by high-capacity leaders that distinguish them from "common leaders" whose attention is diverted by problem-solving and driving toward results. These four habits all relate to the fast-track system in the brain.

R—REMAIN RELATIONAL. Common leaders tend to be problem focused. They are driven by fear of failing to get results and solve problems. Consequently, they value results and solutions more than relationships. This tends to leave them isolated, overwhelmed, and operating out of a motivational system in the brain that virtually guarantees their pace will not be sustainable. RARE leaders have trained themselves to operate from a completely different brain system that we'll look at in a moment. This alternative brain system and the habits that it cultivates help them keep their relationships bigger than their problems.

A—ACT LIKE YOURSELF. As a leader, when I don't know how to act like myself, people don't know what to expect from me. They never know when I'll be angry or sullen, anxious or upbeat. Thus, they learn to walk around me on eggshells as they wait to see which leader they are going to get. RARE leaders have a consistency of character anchored in a positive core identity that lets people know that whatever emotions I may face, I still know how to act like myself.

R—RETURN TO JOY. Perhaps the single biggest factor in producing sustainable motivation is the leader's ability to return to joy from a variety of negative emotions. Leaders who can experience upsetting emotions such as shame, anger, fear, and despair—yet possess the skills to recover quickly and help their people recover as well—are rarely overwhelmed by the situations they face. Groups that learn how to face these emotions and recover collectively grow a strength that can face almost any problem.

E—ENDURE HARDSHIP WELL. In some ways, this is the goal of the whole process. Leaders who learn to suffer well are truly rare. Most of us are doing everything we can to avoid suffering. Our capacity to handle hardship can be thought of as infant, child, adult, parent, and elder-level maturity. Just as a parent can handle more hardship than their child, so an emotionally mature leader can deal with more than one who is a functional child (emotionally speaking).

THE FAST-TRACK SYSTEM IN THE BRAIN

There are two systems in the brain that are often oversimplified as "left brain" and "right brain." The one that is dominant on the left is the **slow-track system.** By using conscious thought, the slow-track system operates more slowly, but it is, of course, what we notice consciously. The slow track is optimized for management. Its primary job is to monitor results and provide explanations and solutions to the problems we face. The slow track gets most of the attention in leadership development.

But did you know that there is a system in the brain that operates faster than conscious thought? We call it the **fast-track** or "master" system. People have known for years that there are things happening in the brain we cannot quite catch consciously. While most people have been looking below consciousness for that activity, we are only now discover-

---

Slow-track System

- Management system
- Slow brain processor (5 Hz)
- Runs at conscious speed
- Left-brain dominant
- Follows master system
  - Manages strategy
  - Solves problems
  - Plans long term
  - Optimizes results

ing there is activity above consciousness. This supra-conscious action does its work faster than we can "keep up" consciously. Its primary job is relational reality. *Who am I in my world* must be clear before I can think about other things. The fast-track system controls how we regulate our emotions, how we remember who we are, who our people are, and how it is like us to act (that is, acting like the self God gave us). In other words, it is our identity center. It controls functions related to:

Fast-track System
• Master system
• Fast brain processor (6 Hz)
• Supra-conscious speed
• Right-brain dominant
• Maintains identity
◦ Individual
◦ Group
• Supplies motivation
◦ Individual
◦ Group
• Optimizes engagement

- Identity
- Motivation
- Emotional control
- Ability to focus
- Relational skills
- Care for others
- Conscience
- Values

The fast track does not listen to the words spoken during classroom study because they move too slowly. Words are work for the slow track. The fast track observes what people are doing. This is why we become aware of people and what they are doing before we start thinking about them. Awareness comes first because awareness is a fast-track activity.

Another example of the difference between slow and fast tracks comes if we compare two everyday tasks—reasoning and face recognition. You are familiar with both experiences from school.

REASONING   **FACE RECOGNITION**

$$X = (25 - 23)(3^2 + 1) + 5$$

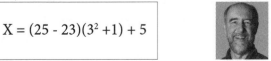

Notice that with one of these familiar tasks you do NOT start by wondering, *How do I figure this out?* Except for people with brain damage, we "know" the picture is a face. Your fast track did the work just now so that by the time your slow track was conscious you already "knew" it was a face. The box on the left was sent to your slow track, where discovering that X equals the number 25 takes much longer. If you tried to teach both tasks to a computer you would soon discover that recognizing a face is actually a much more complex task.

THE FAST TRACK AND RELATIONSHIPS

We tend to classify things that run faster than consciousness as "automatic." Nothing happens automatically in living systems. What we call "automatic" consists of learned processes that run faster than the conscious mind so they are finished before we are aware that they were running. Because they happen faster than consciousness we do not consciously remember learning them, but learn them we did!

What do we generally assume will happen "automatically"? Our identity, motivation, emotional control, ability to focus, relationships, care for others, conscience, and values are some of the forces we expect will show up on their own when we wake up. These are the mind's master processes, and they receive faster processing than conscious thought. We might call this cluster our *identity* or our *emotional or relational competence.*

You can see from the list of functions above that there are quite a few skills that run in the fast track. Since we cannot consciously remember learning these skills we cannot consciously know which skills we learned and which ones we are missing.

As we look around we realize not everyone has the same relational intelligence or ability to handle upsets. We generally assume that others will have the same skills we have. But what did we learn? What are we missing? What skills do the people we lead have? How can we improve emotional intelligence? Leaders have a double task when it comes to the fast-track processes. RARE leaders not only ensure that these seemingly automatic skills run well in themselves but also that these skills develop in their group members. These skills become the core to a group's identity.

We started this section by saying that nothing happens automatically in living systems, but some things are "wired in" so they are almost automatic. The BIG one is that the slow track is wired to automatically follow the fast track. This means that, if leaders get the fast-track relational part right for themselves and their team, the management thinking follows automatically. We get leadership plus management. We have both front tires on the road and steering the car. Focus on building management systems, and leadership is left to chance. Focus on building leadership systems, and you will always improve management. That is automatic.

HOW THIS WORKS IN THE BRAIN

Both the fast track and slow track in the brain can develop habits. To be a good leader you require a diversity of good habits in both fast (leadership) and slow (management) systems. Habits live in the white matter of the brain, and what gives them their power is that white matter runs up to 200 times faster than gray matter.

Fast—faster—fastest

The conscious thought that we have been calling the "slow track" actually operates fairly fast, updating itself with a new state five times every second. Identity processes we have been calling the "fast track" operate even faster, updating six times every second. But this is all gray matter speed. Gray matter is very flexible and can figure out new reality and paths as it goes. However, to keep from getting bogged down, the brain creates "habits" that are prepackaged responses to known situations. Habits take a month or more to grow because the brain has to wrap the habit nerves in white insulation, and that takes some time. Once the habit is properly insulated, that cluster will run up to 200 times faster than gray matter. Habits are the fastest.

When we look at the brain itself we see the outside covered by gray matter doing its flexible best and the inside of the brain cross-connected with white. These fastest connections are present in both the fast-track and slow-track sides of the brain. We have both leadership and management habits for our lives. When things get tough, the one with the most "good habits" wins.

Each habit is a tool or skill. Both the fast and slow tracks develop habits. This book is about developing habits in the fast-track system because that will optimize the slow-track habits as well. The more we practice our skills, the more natural they become until they happen without a conscious deliberation.

Understanding white matter helps us appreciate why habits are so important. They go into operation before our conscious thought engages. People who build fast-track skills into habits operate with

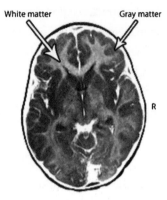

White matter   Gray matter

R

MRI cross section of the brain

greater love, joy, peace, patience, and self-control. Habit qualities seem to happen automatically because they happen faster than we can think about them.

A well-trained fast-track system allows us to return to joy (restore a relationship) quickly from almost any emotion, remain relational during any crisis, and remember how to act like ourselves no matter how we feel. When this system is not well-trained, we will struggle with all of these skills. To compensate, we will be forced to turn to the conscious-thought slow-track system on the left side of the brain.

For example, I (Marcus) recently had a conversation with several pastors who were lamenting how many young people were leaving the church. They zeroed in on how to improve the quality of the ministries designed to attract teens. This management thinking left these leaders stuck in slow-track thinking. As a result, their solutions to the problem of retaining their young adults were all focused on programming. They were tinkering with the problem exclusively from a left-brain-dominant, results-focused, problem-solving perspective.

By looking at the situation from a right-brain-oriented, fast-track perspective, I was able to explain to them that their problem had little to do with programming. The solution was relational. Few of the young people in the church had a relationship with the older folks. Few of the adults, parents, and elders in the church were building relationships with the young people. Consequently, the youth group functioned like an island in the church—disconnected and uninvolved. If you want young people to stay in church, they have to feel like they belong, add value, and feel valued. Which band plays and how relevant your program is have nothing to do with this.

Fast-track skills also influenced how I talked about the problem. I didn't try to shame them and say, "You're all wrong. Here's the real answer!" I didn't get angry or try to scare them by saying, "If you don't do something about this now, it's going to be too late." I started with relational connection. I told them it was clear they cared deeply about their young people and their churches. I also used curiosity as a tool to keep the conversation relational by asking, "I'm curious. Have you looked at this as an issue of community identity and belonging rather than programming?" By the end of the conversation, they all wanted to know more. Our relationships were stronger than when we started.

WHY THIS BRAIN SCIENCE IS IMPORTANT FOR LEADERS

Everyone's master system encounters "road hazards" it cannot manage and "blows a tire" now and then. When people prove hard to lead we tend to start managing them instead of leading them. If our master system shuts down, our mental steering shifts to the management side of the brain and runs at conscious speed. To use our analogy of steering a car, we usually have two tires in front for steering. If one tire goes flat the car will pull very hard to the side. The best solution is to stop and repair the flat tire and not to develop more strategies for driving with one wheel out of commission.

RARE leaders use difficulties as opportunities to focus on improving relational skills before improving task management. When both the leadership and management systems are running well they work well together. Leaders with poorly developed master systems will find themselves operating almost exclusively out of their brain's slow-track system. Results are predictable and almost inevitable. Here are a few to consider:

Mistaking hard work for leadership

As we've already seen, leaders can confuse working with leading. In fact, most leaders reach their positions because they are really good at getting things done. But perhaps this is part of the problem. Working is about getting a job done and there is certainly some of that in leadership. However, *leading is primarily about guiding the group that does the work.*

Focusing on results in ways that damage relationships

I (Marcus) recently had a moment when I got stuck in slow-track mode and forgot to pay attention to that part of my brain that helps me act like myself. It is a simple story but might help to illustrate what this looks like. I took a short trip to pick up my father-in-law, who has Alzheimer's. He had wandered away from the house and walked nearly a mile to church. It was a Tuesday afternoon but he got disoriented and thought it was Sunday morning. As I was driving to get him, I was completely in the conscious-thought part of my brain. I was busy problem-solving in my mind trying to decide what we were going to do to keep this sort of thing from happening again. I was also focused on the task of picking him up. I felt alone solving my problem.

Because I was focused on how to manage my father-in-law, I neglected the fast-track system in my brain that would remind me of how it is like me to act in a situation like this. As a result, I helped my father-in-law into the car and drove off, never thinking of the pastor who had found my father-in-law and called me to come get him. I realized later (once I got back in touch with the relational part of my brain), that there was a whole community keeping an eye on my father-in-law. The pastor probably had to waste time and energy looking and wondering where my father-in-law had gone now. Had

I had picked him up or had he had wandered off again? Not a huge problem, but still, my focus on managing the problem made me forget to lead the group that was helping me. I later called the pastor, passing it off as my absentminded behavior, and apologized for the inconvenience I must have caused him.

Forgetting our group identity and acting in isolation may seem like a small thing. But small things like this damage relationships. Loss of trust by others happens all the time to leaders who fixate on problem-solving at the cost of relational skills. Leaders often solve problems and get results but frustrate people along the way.

Slow-track thinking can come to define whole organizations. I (Marcus) know several people who worked for one of the largest churches in America. It was a well-organized machine that got amazing results. However, it had a reputation for "chewing up and spitting out" staff members. The driven, type-A culture the organization promoted definitely got results, but it also left a wake of broken relationships.

Burnout is typical of organizations led by results-oriented, problem-solving leaders. These leaders have a well-trained management brain, but often lack a well-trained relational brain. If the master system is untrained or misfiring, the "successful" leader will drive herself and her group toward anxiety, anger, depression, and burnout. In the end, this results-focused leader will produce a structure that is likely to come to a grinding halt or a spectacular crash.

Wearing themselves out

One morning as I (Jim) read Paul's admonition in Galatians 6:9, "Let us not become weary in doing good," I thought to myself, "That is easy for you to say! I already feel really tired and it isn't even afternoon." I might have added that my work was not as draining as dealing with the workers with whom I shared the tasks. Perhaps, you can relate.

Of course, I was missing the main point of the text. Rather than telling me not to feel tired (which is something even Jesus couldn't avoid), *Paul was encouraging me to persist in doing what was good and not allow my weariness with poor results to change my course.* It is easy to grow weary in well doing when I am not seeing results or when the people are questioning whether the results are worth the effort. At times the discouragement comes from seeing the gap between where I know I should be and the reality of where I am. That morning I was just a tired visionary wondering how long I could sustain the effort and keep others going as well. (Can you relate?)

> I got more things done than most people I know, but I was exhausted from working like a dog.

Hard work and anxiety were wearing me out, but most of it was self-generated—still working while others were home watching TV. I got more things finished than most people I know, but I was exhausted from working like a dog. I was also struggling with a sense of anxiety that was burning up all my excess energy and robbing me of rest.

When I discovered what we call the RARE lifestyle, things began to turn around. In new ways, I was able to keep my motivation strong, fresh, and positive. Learning to maintain my fast-track system changed my life. Discovering and using the highest-grade motivation available not only helped me recover quickly from the weariness that would set in, it helped me guide others to keep a rewarding pace that allowed them to add their creativity and energy to our mission. I have seen the crushing lifestyle that I once lived get the better of some of the most powerful leaders I have known. In fact, far too many leaders and the groups who follow them are drawing their motivation from the wrong power source. As a result, they are running on fumes and wondering how much longer they can go on.

Creating a culture of fear

When problem solving gets all of our focus as an organization, it breeds a level of fear in everything we do. "What will happen if we don't solve this problem? What will we do if we don't get these results?"

One of the biggest frauds in the business world in 2015 occurred at Volkswagen when it was discovered that they had intentionally designed software that made the emissions on their diesel cars appear cleaner than they actually were. This deception grew from a fear culture. Employees and management were afraid to admit they could not meet the extremely high goals set by the corporation's top executives. The corporate culture was such that cheating and lying seemed preferable to looking bad to the boss.[5]

Leaders who lack the RARE skills that characterize a well-trained fast-track system will eventually create malfunctioning groups. The leader's shortcomings impact the entire organization, generating a fear-based culture where people are afraid to admit failure or expose weakness.

LESS TIRED, MORE JOYFUL

Leaders have a double task when it comes to the fast-track processes in that they not only need these automatic skills to run well in themselves but they must be working in their group as well. Great leaders continue improving and diversifying everyone's relational skills. What we notice consciously is how highly motivated, joyful, engaged, and satisfied their group seems to be.

Outstanding leaders almost never know the brain science behind their efforts, but they sense the importance of what they often call "character." Many leaders are guided and motivated by spiritual beliefs and biblical practices. What creates RARE leaders is that they have the skills that go with the beliefs and know how to pass those skills to others.

The RARE leaders we try to emulate use this faster, more powerful engine so they are less tired, less concerned about results, less fatigued, more joyful, more peaceful, and more admired while producing people who are resilient even in hard times. RARE leaders can stay the course without unnecessarily exhausting themselves and others.

Our book is written in two sections. The next few chapters (2–5) will discuss how the process of training the fast track works, reasons it has remained hidden for so long, how the leader's brain works, and how fast-track leadership develops.

Some readers will want to go directly to the second section (chapters 6–11), where we lead you though the practices that develop the four RARE leadership skills. This chapter may have answered your questions for now, so choose the reading path that works best for you.

In addition, we've included a special Brain Science section at the end of each chapter, diving deeper into some of the physical and theoretical bases of the book. Feel free to skim over these if they're not your thing, but exploring these ideas will give you a more robust understanding of the concepts we're discussing and how you can benefit.

Brain Science for RARE Leadership

The MASTER Fast-Track Processor

The executive control center is at the very top of our brain but not the top of our head. As the spinal cord grows into our skull pre-birth it goes first to the top, then bends forward to the front of the skull where it turns once

Executive Control Center

Orbital / Prefrontal Cortex

Right Hemisphere

more and ends up just above our eyes and almost where it started. The brain has two sides and the executive control center is on the right side.

Nerve activity enters the brain near the bottom and is "carried" to the top about six times per second in the right brain. Each sweep assembles a "picture" of who and where we are at the moment (provided we are awake). The main focus of this mental picture is answering the question of how to act like myself based on my identity as an individual and "tribe." Because each sweep is completed in less time than it takes to become conscious (one fifth of a second) we call this process the "fast track." The speed of the fast track ensures that we always remember who we are without stopping to figure it out but, at the same time, makes all the fast-track functions "transparent" and "automatic" to conscious thought.

Every time a sweep of the fast track is completed successfully the final picture is assembled in the executive control center at the top known as the prefrontal cortex (PFC). Some VERY important things only happen in the PFC. Here is a partial list of exclusive PFC functions:

- Identity (what do I and my people do under these conditions)
- Personal preferences (what values reflect who I am)
- Creativity
- Judging if an activity was satisfying (did this get me where I wanted to go)
- Goal-directed behavior
- Moral and social behavior
- Correcting our incorrect interpretations of others
- Comparing how I am doing over time
- Calming upsets in myself and others
- Trust (knowing when to trust a face)
- Figuring the least damaging solution
- Predicting a negative outcome
- Moment-by-moment updating of a situation
- How stressed I become (including the level of stress hormones in my body)
- Curiosity
- Feeling appreciation

By checking exclusive functions like curiosity and feeling appreciation we can easily test if the fast track up to the PFC is running well at the moment.

Clearly these skills are all crucial to leadership and full engagement by groups. Without enough training in the full range of relational skills, the fast track cramps up before it reaches the top. Every time incoming reality fails to reach the PFC the skills in the bullet points shut down. Leadership stops and the rest of the brain careens along. Without executive control by the PFC we resort to rules, problem solving, and avoiding pain. The brain forgets relationships, identity, and the abilities listed above.

Focusing on behavior consistent with our identity is the best way to enlist the highest executive functions of the brain. The skills required to be emotionally mature are taught in the Bible and clarified through brain science. As you continue through this book, you will learn how these skills impact the way we lead and some practical ways to grow your own.

DISCUSSION QUESTIONS

1. Have you ever known a leader who excelled at the RARE habits described in this chapter? How would you describe that person and their impact on the group they led?

2. Would you say that you operate more out of the slow track or the fast track of your brain in your leadership activity? How do you understand the difference?

3. Describe your leadership training/mentoring. Was it primarily focused on slow-track management and problem-solving skills or on fast-track relational skills?

4. Which leader has had the most impact on your development? How would you rate them in the four RARE skills introduced here?

SECTION 1

Understanding Fast-Track Leadership

CHAPTER 2

The Difference Between RARE Leaders and Sandbox Leaders

Learning from the worst cases

WHAT HAPPENS WHEN leaders *don't* lead with emotional intelligence? When they neglect building those "fast-track," more relational leadership habits?

Probably most of us somewhere along the line have experienced the destruction such leaders leave in their wake. *Harvard Business Review* coined the term "sandbox leadership"—which, they say, is epidemic.

> *In the past few months we've seen [childish attitudes] reflected in the halls of government and corporate boardrooms across the country. Arrogance, pouting, tantrums, personal attacks, and betrayal of trust seem to be the order of the day. Situations at [some large, well-known corporations] demonstrate the kind of sandbox leadership that is all too prevalent right now. The timing could not be worse. The nation's current problems, as vast and overwhelming as they are, appear secondary to the whims of spoiled children, unwilling to play well together. At a time when we need solid, grounded leadership more than ever, we seem to be in short supply of adults who act like, well . . . like adults.*[1]

Sandbox leaders are grown-ups in positions of responsibility whose lack of emotional maturity creates catastrophic consequences for their unsuspecting followers. The higher a person rises in leadership circles, the more devastating the impact of sandbox leadership can be.

- Churches split
- Affairs occur
- Leaders burn out
- Boards feud with staff
- A trail of wounded people gets left in the dust

All of these crises and more can be traced back to leaders who are competent and charismatic but lack emotional maturity. The current crisis in leadership relates directly to the lack of mature, fast-track skills in leaders throughout our corporations, nonprofits, churches, and government structures. Fast-track skills, as we noted in chapter 1, are the relational habits in the brain that run faster than we can follow consciously. Mature individuals have developed a wide variety of fast-track skills for leading when things go wrong and upset the team. Sandbox leaders become children under pressure.

The first leadership book I (Marcus) ever read was John Maxwell's *21 Irrefutable Laws of Leadership*. Law #1 was called the "law of the lid." Leaders cannot rise above the level of their capability. Through years of leading and talking to other leaders, I have become convinced that the number one lid on most leaders is emotional immaturity.

To lead well, we need a new paradigm. That is precisely what we will be presenting in this chapter.

Discovering how the brain operates changes the way we look at emotions, relationships, and maturity, and reveals keys for personal and corporate transformation. For Christian leaders it is especially insightful that these discoveries in brain science are confirming lessons the Bible has taught for years.

REPENT!

Stephen Covey has been an influential guide to leaders for several decades. In his book *The 8th Habit: From Effectiveness to Greatness*, he talks about the power of paradigms.

*If you want to make minor, incremental changes and improve-
ments, work on practices, behavior or attitude. But if you want to
make significant, quantum improvement, work on paradigms.*[2]

The term "paradigm shift" came from the philosopher Thomas
Kuhn's 1962 book, *The Structure of Scientific Revolutions*, where he
argued that new facts did little to change how people think. We
needed a change of viewpoint. Changing viewpoints is what Jesus
meant by the word we translate "repent," which in Greek means seeing things a whole new way.

Paradigms explain how things work. When we believed that bad
blood made us sick, we thought bleeding patients would make them
better. Germ theory was an entirely new paradigm, and it took medi-
cine a good long time to "repent" and see things a new way. With a new
explanation of how things worked came new ways of solving problems.
Doctors changed from black coats to hide the blood to white coats to
show they were germ-free—at least symbolically. Until this paradigm
change, doctors found washing their hands between patients an
annoying and inefficient way to work.

Nowhere does the difference between RARE leaders and
management-based leaders show up more clearly than in how problems are solved. For leaders, problems are almost always "people
problems" and leadership skill involves transforming the way people
participate. This paradigm of how people function will determine
our understanding of 1) what can change and 2) what will achieve
that change. For Western leadership this generally means we provide better information so people make better choices and things will
change. Isn't that how things work?

THIN AIR AND A LESSON IN CULTURAL DIFFERENCES

I (Jim) was traveling in the Himalayas and looking for ways to train
businesspeople in developing their relational skills. We also planned to
use the same skill training to reduce the alcohol and addiction problems in the workforce. To the Western mind, this makes sense. But

there in the mountains I encountered an interesting paradigm: There was no change expected during a lifetime. Changes happen between incarnations, and people work toward "better luck next life." The culture had no stories of people who overcame obstacles, no shipping clerks that worked their way up to business owners, and no expectation that choice had anything to do with changing our current existence. The idea of addiction recovery seemed to vanish in thin air—but then, the air is thin up there. Paradigms are powerful.

Better information, better choices?

The traditional paradigm that has dominated Western thought for the last four hundred years can be summed up in a simple equation:

Reason + Good Choices = Transformation

This paradigm grew out of the Enlightenment. When René Decartes uttered his famous phrase, "*Cogito ergo sum*" ("I think, therefore I am"), he started a revolution in philosophy that believed the most important thing about being human was our ability to reason. The British philosophers took this a step further and argued that people are molded by the choices they make. According to these thinkers, choices built on reason (as opposed to superstition, or faith, or revelation) were the best choices. These academics taught a philosophical theory called *voluntarism*, from which we get our equation "reason + good choices = transformation." The English brought this very rational idea to the colonies, where it took root and since then underlies many of our assumptions about "how things work"—including in the church.

> The assumption has been that people need to be told what to do, then forced to report on what they're doing, or nothing will change.

The idea is that if you give people good information, they can make good choices and change their lives. Most preaching and most discipleship programs are built around this philosophy. Of course, as most preachers can tell you, just giving people good information doesn't guarantee that they will make good choices or guarantee real life change is going to occur. In fact, in both ministry and business we take it for granted that good information *doesn't* necessarily lead to good choices, so we add another element in the hopes of producing changed behavior—accountability.

WHY ACCOUNTABILITY DOESN'T WORK

More than once, I (Marcus) have been asked by a ministry leader to develop a discipleship program with some "teeth" in it. By this they mean discipleship that is strong on accountability. Most pastors have figured out that simply telling people what is wise doesn't mean they are going to do it. So, the assumption is that people need to be told what to do, then forced to report on how they are doing, or nothing will change.

The accountability solution has ruled the business world as well. Voluntarists believe that if we want to see change (either personally or corporately), we need to inform people of how we want them to behave, get them to commit to adopting that behavior, then hold them accountable to their commitment. (See: performance reviews.) It is virtually a given that any book on leadership will say accountability is the key to transformation.

As widespread and apparently sensible as the accountability solution has become, it has proven to be a massive failure at producing the results it promises. Nearly all discipleship and leadership training we provide our pastors and corporate managers is based on accountability. Yet when we look at the fruit, we see a long history of fallen leaders, relational train wrecks, and discouraged followers.

One of the reasons the accountability paradigm falls short is that the model is fueled by fear. When I meet with my accountability group, I am only happy to see them if I have been successful in keeping my promises. If I have failed, there is fear in the meeting. I am afraid to disappoint the group. I am afraid to fall short of expectations. I am afraid of the consequences of my failure. More than one accountability group has fallen apart because people simply stopped coming when they started failing.

IDENTITY, BELONGING, AND TRANSFORMATION

Choice runs in the "slow track" of our brain. What, then, runs in the fast track that has executive control? The answer is *identity*. *Who we are determines what we will do* and identity operates faster and more powerfully than choices. Identity's power over choice does not fit our rational mindset. In addition, our brain thinks of who we are not only as an individual but as a group identity as well. Group and individual identities are not the same but they also cannot be separated. I always understand myself in reference to others like me. I am a woman, a carpenter, a Cubs fan, a Canadian, or a leader according to my group identity.

The four RARE habits of exceptional leaders are built around identity and belonging. The power of these two key ingredients, missing in the old paradigm, cannot be exaggerated.

R – Remain relational (belonging)
A – Act like yourself (identity)
R – Return to joy (being glad to be together)
E – Endure hardships well (using hard times to bring us closer)

Belonging and identity also provide the real keys to transformation. When accountability groups work, most of the time it is a byproduct of good group leadership. Strong relationships are formed, a sense of belonging develops, and a positive identity emerges that produces real life change. The more pronounced these identity elements are, the more lasting the transformation. If we were to reduce this solution to a formula, it would be:

Identity + Belonging = Transformation

Lasting transformation takes place when a person's identity changes and that person becomes comfortable in living out of their new identity. The best coaches, pastors, teachers, managers, and leaders are the ones who instill a clear sense of identity into their group and help people understand "This is who we are and this is how it is like us to act." (You will be hearing this statement again in this book. It's central to RARE leadership.)

"I DON'T BELONG WITH THESE PEOPLE": LOUIS'S STORY

Louis and Anna Kang are young church planters in an immigrant, multiethnic community of central Los Angeles. Louis graduated from a prestigious Canadian university and came to California for seminary. As he jogged around the neighborhoods he realized how insular the islands were for every ethnic group. Looking into churches, he realized that the same divisions existed between church communities. Louis set out to create a church that could bridge cultures and prioritize relationships. He shared one example of a church where relationships were not prioritized in the midst of difficulty:

> *The financial numbers and the membership of the church dropped drastically and hard decisions had to be made. The one indelible mark of this process was that relationships were secondary. Accusations, mistrust, hurt, factions, people being blamed and accused; in short, people were desperate to point the finger. Anxiety overload, enormous pressure to crunch the right numbers, incessant talk of filling the seats, contemptuousness—the list was long and wearisome. I realized in planting our new church that this was not a model we wanted to replicate.*

But his church planting effort soon ran up against the reality that immigrant communities in Los Angeles are often quite poor. For Louis and his family, this meant either going on food stamps or abandoning the mission. Sitting before the food stamp interviewer with his master's degree, his wife, Anna, with two master's degrees and a PhD in process, and being asked what real job skills he had was humiliating. Standing in the line for his stamps, Louis looked in front and behind him and thought, "I don't belong with these people." At that moment, Louis realized he now understood Los Angeles and the problem in the church. *We don't belong with these people. They are not our people.* Louis now says:

> *I believe I am called to plant a church where all people belong. I desire to plant a church where relationships and an identity come*

to the forefront. I remember my coach stopped me and gave some great advice. He said lead through your relationships. I began to understand that leading was more about relationships that fostered trust and emerged from trust. I am beginning to trust the strength of friendships without ignoring the benchmarks of progress.

IDENTITY AND THE FAST TRACK

As our fast-track brain system assembles who we are in the world this instance (remember, six pictures a second) it creates a mental map of our important relationships and experiences that can help us know how to live here. The pictures are quite different when facing an angry boss or sitting on our grandparents' porch on a summer evening. What the fast track provides in both situations is a picture of who we are and how that fits with the people around us. By considering the possible interactions (and the fast track quickly runs simulations of many scenarios) we develop motivation and our initial response to any situation. What we need to know for this chapter is that the fast track creates motivation from the mental interaction of our identity with the identity of the group around us. *There is always an individual and a group identity in the picture.*

> The group identity urge is so strong in the brain that adults will die to preserve that identity.

In a very immature brain (similar to children twelve and younger) my objective is always to serve my individual identity. As brains mature (similar to thirteen and over) the goal of serving my group identity has the possibility to develop. The group identity urge is so strong in the brain that adults will die to preserve that identity. (Example: suicide bombers.) Early Christians were willing to see themselves and their children tortured to death by Rome because identities are that powerful. It was not what the early church believed, but who they loved, that created this willingness to face death. They died to maintain their individual and group identity.

ANNA: RETRAINING THE BRAIN WITH JOY

Both group and individual identities can be powered by fear or by joy. In joy we are glad to be together. In fear we watch out for threats together. Pastor Louis's wife, Anna, had earned her graduate degrees in counseling. Anna herself had come to the US from Korea when she was young and lived through a long series of stepmothers. She didn't find anywhere she belonged. As a teenager she became a Christian because she was told that becoming a Christian would change her life from bad to good.

The good Christian life didn't happen, so Anna looked for a group that was more serious about their faith and found a strong leader who was downright intense in her beliefs. However, this group identity proved to be built on fear, so while the group became very loyal to the leader, the level of trust between members stayed low. Their distrust of outsiders was even stronger and their fear of the devil was higher still. One tragic day the leader beat a member to death, attempting to remove an evil spirit, and they all ended up in prison.

For the better part of a year, loyalty and fear kept them in prison, as no one was willing to testify. Eventually the women began to talk, realizing they had all been abused in various ways. As they faced their shame they also were freed to speak and were released from their literal prison cells.

Anna went on to study Christian counseling, receive counseling herself, learn inner healing, and minister to others—but her own emotional life with her husband and children remained out of control. Anna had trained her slow track every way she knew how, but her fast-track identity regularly shut down when it ran out of skills or into bad memories. It is hard to be a pastor's wife, church planter, and mother when you are trying to choose the right thing to do but you are riding on a bucking bronco of emotions. Your will seems to shut down every time you could really use the help. Anna continued looking for the life that being a Christian was supposed to bring. It was then she discovered that she had a fast track that could be trained.

Anna was at a training session led by Jim and his wife, Kitty, when she learned that joy could retrain the brain. She asked to see Kitty and at that meeting she told Kitty, "I don't have much time or money but I have an hour. Teach me the fast-track skills." Five years of training later, Anna coauthored *Joyful Journey* with Jim and two of her friends. She trains leaders in their growing church plant and teaches with Louis in a Hispanic Bible school. Louis will tell you that because of what they have learned in poverty and weakness they have become more effective leaders than from their combined degrees. Louis and Anna are keeping out of the sandbox and developing RARE skills.

> There are street bullies and there are benevolent bullies.

JOY, FEAR, AND FUELING THE POWER PLANT

We could say that identity produces the strongest power plant for any kind of action or even resistance to action. Identity does not figure very strongly in the rationalist mindset of voluntarism. Many of us, believing that good information will result in good choices, wonder what could motivate a suicide bomber. What has that kind of power?

Extremists of all religions (and to a lesser degree, gangs and cults) depend on fast-track identity for a power plant. The fuel used to run this power plant in terrorist or radical behavior is fear. Fear is explosive motivating fuel. RARE leadership uses the same power plant but a different and more powerful fuel. The fuel of the fast-track identity in RARE leadership is *joy*. Joy is a far less explosive fuel than fear but more powerful still. With fear as a motivator we get predators: Hitler, Stalin, Mao, ISIS, and urban street gangs. With joy as a motivating fuel we get protectors: Jesus, Mandela, Martin Luther King Jr., Mother Teresa, and RARE leadership. Changing fuels is a key to transformation. Here is how it looks with the two fast-track fuels:

Fast-track fuel	With Identity	Without Identity
Joy	**RARE Power plant**	Party time
Fear	**Religious Radical**	Bully

Joy + Identity = RARE power plant
Joy (no identity) = Party time
Fear + Identity = Terrorist/Religious radical
Fear + (no identity) = Bully

It is worth noting that there are street bullies and there are benevolent bullies (like those that Louis encountered in the megachurch), but either way they leave us feeling very beat up. Joy without identity looks like the program in way too many churches. Fear without identity looks like the environment in way too many schools and workplaces.

"WE'RE GOING TO LOVE YOU JUST THE WAY YOU ARE AND DO OUR BEST TO HELP YOU FIND JESUS"

As we will explore in the next chapter, neurological research has made it clear that the human brain was designed for joy. Our fast-track guidance functions operate best when powered by joy. From the bottom to the top, the brain is a joy-seeking machine and seeks joy above every other human experience. When I make changes in my life because I want to be the person God created me to be, I am making those changes out of the joy that comes from acting like myself and bringing a smile to the faces of "my people." Instead of making changes out of fear of what others will think or say or do, I make changes because of who I am and the joy it brings to my group.

A church where I (Marcus) have done a lot of training provides a classic example of the two paradigms discussed in this chapter. On the one hand, the leaders of the recovery ministry at this church have built a wonderful culture in which the weak and strong interact on a regular basis. Nearly three hundred people gather most weeks to worship and then split into support groups where they learn, heal, and pray with trained lay ministers.

Every time I visit this church, I am impressed with the level of belonging that has been created in this group and the clear identity that says, "We're going to love you just the way you are and do our best to help you find Jesus." Members of this recovery group often visit each other's homes, meet at restaurants, and look for one another at church. The strong (those who are reaching out to the people looking for help) connect with those more fragile. Hurting people from all walks of life are included in the fellowship. I've met strippers, alcoholics, bikers, battered women, and hardcore metal heads at these events. Many have seen their lives transformed as they have grown more connected.

On the other hand, the leadership team at the church had not built the same type of culture. Instead, isolation, distrust, and fear of a powerful, very successful pastor created a toxic leadership environment. The growth and "success" of the church masked the low-joy leadership and its tensions to most observers. Leaders were held to high levels of accountability inside this group, but one got the sinking feeling that the accountability was just one more way for the pastor to stay in control of (manage) everything that went on in his church.

The contrast could not have been greater between the two groups. One of them blew up and nearly destroyed the church. The other one served as a rock through the hard transitions that followed. Can you figure out which group thrived and which barely survived?

WHY WE IGNORE THE FAST TRACK

If fast-track solutions are so superior to slow-track, conscious choices, why have we never heard about this amazing part of our brain? Three reasons: voluntarism, the speed of the fast track, and the fact that the slow track does not monitor the fast without special training.

As we have seen, voluntarism is a paradigm or set of lenses that says everything important for humans is in the conscious, thinking track. How things work, how Christians should believe and behave, and how to solve problems are all there under the will. But the fast track is not there, so we will never see it by looking into conscious thought.

Supra-conscious speed is only six cycles per second as compared to five for the conscious processor, but that is enough so that every time we gather a conscious picture our fast track is already gone. Since we never consciously "see" the fast track there we don't remember that it was present. We revert to terms like: instinctive reaction, intuition, automatic response, and "I was born this way" to explain what we then ignore.

The conscious mind is wired like a puppy on a leash to follow the identity and reality of the fast track. As such, the slow track does not have any way to monitor whether the fast track is running or not. The slow track just goes on as though the fast-track business is always being done. When the fast track shuts down due to limited habits (lacking maturity skills), the management system simply wanders off managing all of life—unless it has been trained to notice signs that the boss has passed out. There are tests that can be run to see if the fast track is running, procedures that can be followed to get the fast track running again. These tests and "reset procedures" are the most special tools of the RARE leader. There will be more on ways to test and reset in the following chapter.

IDENTITY GROUPS: BUILDING A TEAM OF ALLIES

In keeping with the RARE paradigm, rather than relying on accountability groups to change behavior, we recommend identity groups. Whereas an accountability group asks people to get together and be honest about their behavior and whether they are living up to their commitments, an identity group is focused on helping people remember who they are and how it is like them to act—how God created them to act.

> In our group we don't try to fix one another. We call out what is best in one another.

As leaders we need to have some place where we can take off our mask and show our weakness. We need people around who will protect us in our weak state long enough to heal and grow. We need people who remind us of who we are. Identity groups call out what is best in us and help us act like our redeemed selves.

I (Jim) have been in an identity group with several colleagues over the years. It is not an accountability group in that we do not evaluate each other's behavior or urge faithfulness to a set of promises. Rather, it is a place where we can talk about our struggles and be honest about our issues. We don't try to fix each other. However, we do validate the emotions involved and call out what is best in one another. We will often help each other seek God's presence and peace related to our situation.

I (Marcus) have recently begun building an identity group with a few close friends (though we are spread out across the country). It is not uncommon to text or to call one another to discuss issues we are facing. Last year, I had found myself in a battle with anxiety. My friends in this group spent many hours listening to me talk through my struggle. I was surprised how many of them had their own stories of significant anxiety. It was comforting to know I wasn't alone. Several of them were able to offer good advice that made a significant difference. They never judged me. Instead, they helped me find God in the midst of the mess. They gave me advice, and left the door open anytime I needed to process more about my issues. At other times, I would listen to them share about what they were going through. Our goal was always the same: validate the emotions involved, and help the person move toward a place of peace.

IDENTITY AND INTIMACY

Here is the paradox of belonging and identity. All human group identities are, in a sense, "deformed" because we are fallen human beings. The RARE paradigm only works because we continually seek to bring our individual and group identities to a higher standard that, as Christians, we see in the life of Jesus. We see His life as a human as a model of the higher standard.

But here is where our brains can limit understanding. The slow-track part of our brains can analyze information about the life of Jesus and be inspired by it, but by itself, the slow track cannot change our identity. Simply knowing the truth about how Jesus modeled godliness does not make us godly. For example, Isaiah knew that God was holy, but it was not until he encountered this transcendent God that his identity changed. Interacting with a holy God made Isaiah aware of his own sinfulness and, interacting with a holy God healed and transformed him.

The good news here is that God has not stopped interacting with the human race. In the words of Francis Schaeffer, "He is there and He is not silent." The fast track of the brain is not oriented toward words, and God does not interact with this part of our brain with words. What He does is deeper than words. This is why so many pastors and Christians speak of being "led," "guided," or "prompted" by God. They are trying to describe a nonverbal experience of the presence of God in their lives.

How often have pastors told their people, "The Lord laid this message on my heart," or "I felt led by God to deal with this issue today"? In brain science terms, the idea of being led by the Lord is another way of saying that God interacts with the nonverbal, fast-track part of our brains at a level that is deeper than words alone can reach.

Having said this, there is a role for the slow track. It helps to take a look at how we sense God is leading and guiding and put what we are experiencing into words. This doesn't mean that those words are from God, but it does mean that we can put into words how we feel we are being led.

Interaction with a personal God who is there and is not silent is crucial to helping us overcome deformities in our identity. This type of intimacy with God is a hallmark of emotionally mature leaders who pay attention to their fast-track habits.

PAULO: WEAKNESS AND TRANSFORMATION

There probably aren't a lot of leadership books talking about how to handle weakness. However, our approach to weakness defines us as leaders. Sandbox leaders hide their own weaknesses and either attack or enable the weaknesses of others. RARE leaders are honest about their own weaknesses and build communities in which the weak and strong interact regularly (as we saw with the recovery group). We'll have a lot more to say about this in the chapter on Acting Like Yourself.

Paulo and Ieda were missionary leaders and trainers who everyone loved. Paulo had people skills, style, and a winning personality. His smile and warmth made strangers feel at home from the first moment,

> Strong people who are good at hiding their weaknesses like to hang out together.

and his energy seemed endless. Paulo was a man of vision and soon became a leader, training missionaries and leading teams. Yet everything Paulo knew and taught to others did not stop him from the affair that took him out of the sky like a duck that flies over a hunter.

As Paulo rebuilt his marriage and family, he took the RARE path of accepting his weakness as his issue. He entered a program for sexual addiction; but quite unlike most leaders, Paulo began to use his affair as a way to teach others how to deal with their own weaknesses. Instead of hiding his sexual addiction, as most leaders would do, Paulo took the path of learning all he could and teaching others very openly about weaknesses in their lives.

When Paulo discovered the Life Model he was already well into sobriety from his sexual addiction. Paulo says, "The transformation in my life would not be possible without the Holy Spirit and the help of Ieda."

However, Paulo's leadership and ministry immediately disappeared when the affair was discovered. In Brazil there is no recovery from public shame as a leader. When leaders model ways to hide weakness rather than ways to heal and grow, shame and the fear of shame begin to rule. What Paulo learned from the Life Model was how to return to joy from the shame of his affair and teach this to others. We will explain how the fast track returns to joy in a later chapter and how you can develop this habit as well.

Many leaders would want to hide and use a false name if they talk about a weakness. Paulo Henrique Eufrazio Da Silva puts his name on his story because he has found his true identity and is ready to lead others to transformation. This is the mark of a RARE leader.

THE TRANSFORMATION OF A FEARED APARTHEID LEADER

The typical scenario in most groups is that the strong cluster together and the weak are left to fend for themselves. What generally passes for strength is actually based in insecurity and fear. Strength is often a cluster of management skills employed to manage our own image. Many strong people have excellent maturity and people skills but are powered by fear and not by joy. The result is that we have become excellent manipulators and controllers but are isolated in our own fabrication. Our identities manage people but we are not their people and they are not ours.

Strong people who are good at hiding their weaknesses like to hang out together. They invite each other over for dinner. Their children play together, and they usually end up running the church together. Over time, the only people in their circle are other strong people with well-hidden weaknesses. This lifestyle becomes a comfort zone that works against transformation. At the same time there is usually a lot of talk about truth and choice. The stronger people simply make better choices.

Perhaps an example will help us see how changing the fuel of our fast-track thinking from fear to belonging can create transformation. Adriaan Vlok was the head of the Law and Order Ministry of South Africa in the last days of apartheid. In the late 1980s Vlok was one of the most feared men in the country. The *BBC News Hour* ran a special story about him, but it wasn't his brutality that made headlines. It was his transformation. Today, he shares his home with a black family and distributes food to poor families.

Adriaan Vlok took a new look at his identity from Christ's perspective and found it evil and lacking in love. He discovered in Christ's command that he was designed to love others and care for the poor, and this led him out of his comfort zone in a dramatic way. Today, he lives with a joy he never knew as one of the most powerful leaders in the apartheid regime. He has found a home and a new group identity with those he persecuted. Adriaan has been transformed.

The rational mindset would say that Vlok found truth and made better choices. But the RARE mindset would view Vlok as transformed by seeing his strengths as weakness. Through interaction with God and learning to live in a whole new family he grew a new group identity. Changing his fuel from fear to joy also changed Vlok's identity.

Transformation is created when the weak and the strong interact with one another in a culture in which they can share a common identity and a common sense of belonging. This path to developing trust is found in Paul's ideal of the church. Paul envisioned a church in which masters and slaves, rich and poor, Jews and Gentiles, wise and foolish all shared a common identity around the Lord's Table. Such a community brings together the most powerful elements of a transformative culture. It creates a new identity. It provides a place to belong. It gets the strong out of their comfort zones and provides a path to maturity for the weak. We will examine the engine that drives this transformation in the next chapter.

HOW CHANGE HAPPENS

Perhaps it is becoming clear why a leader who wants to see real change or stay on course needs RARE skills—which enhance the development of our "fast track" brain system.

When we leave the development of our fast track to chance we fail to mature and so we fail to lead under pressure. We stay comfortable and keep our weaknesses hidden because, like everyone else, we don't know what to do about weakness that won't go away, even when we know the truth and try to make the right choices. We find new answers are possible when we change the paradigm we use to explain how change works. RARE leadership comes from understanding how to build our identities as individuals and groups. The rest of this book is devoted to showing us how.

Brain Science for RARE Leadership

Individual identity and group identity
in the fast track

The brain's master system has headquarters on the right side and runs many functions: the immune system, focusing attention, setting priorities for each moment, and deciding when we should change our opinions. But the most significant aspect of the fast track is building an effective identity.

Who am I?

Who is my identity group?

What is it like us to do right now under these conditions?

These three priorities are at the core of what the master system is wired to consider.

If we consider these three brain priorities from the negative side we discover that trauma and post-traumatic stress (PTSD) disrupt the brain's ability to answer the questions "Who am I right now and what is it like me and my people to do under these conditions?" No sooner is our identity center disrupted than all attention turns to problems and how to make them stop.

A mature and well-developed fast track needed for leaders responds very differently to stress. Instead of trying to stop the problems, the mature brain keeps our identity, goals, objectives, team, and purpose focused on what is most important. Once we are acting like ourselves we release maximum creativity and the energy needed to solve these problems. We reach important goals with the least possible damage along the way. When leaders keep a clear group identity in place it brings out these creative and focused efforts from the group they lead. Relationships stay more important than problems.

The executive prefrontal cortex at the top of the fast track continues to grow individual and group identities with each day's experience as long as we stay relational. When the executive is OFF and problems become the focus, the executive learns little to nothing from the experience. The fast track learns and becomes more sophisticated when it is ON and relational.

DISCUSSION QUESTIONS

1. Have you known any "sandbox leaders"? What characterized them? What was it like to work with them?

2. Which story in this chapter resonated most strongly with you? In what ways?

3. How have you seen the accountability model fail in churches? What do you think would work better?

4. Would you say your identity is driven more by fear or by joy? How does the fuel that powers your identity change your approach to leadership?

5. How does your identity impact your attitude toward weakness? Why is this so important for a leader?

CHAPTER 3

The Elevator in Your Brain

Building your emotional competence

JIM MARTINI (whom you met in the Introduction) is a business executive who constantly learns ways to improve. He trains his fast track for the best efficiency. When I (Jim) met Martini I named him "the optimizer." Martini optimized his sales, his fitness, his income, and himself. He says:

> *First I learned I could manage time, next I learned I could manage feelings, then I learned "at the end of the day don't ask if you did it all, ask if what you did do was more important than what you didn't do," next I learned that managing time wasn't enough but managing energy was also important. Often we have the time but not the energy.*
>
> *Early in my career, I was introduced to time management. But my paradigm was still using my time efficiently to get it all done. I'm a creative, ambitious guy, so "all" was always a lot. I was the first guy into the office in the morning and the last guy out at night.*
>
> *When our children were in high school two things happened at once. I had just taken over as the national account manager on the Kaiser Permanente account (that's a huge health-care system) for Siemens (the global engineering company), so the possibilities and the demands on my time had grown well beyond my ability to manage.*

And the thought occurred to me that our children would be leaving for college soon and I really needed to get even better at managing my time so that I could spend time with them before they were gone.

A good friend had introduced me to The Seven Habits of Highly Effective People. *Covey's ideas really resonated with me. I learned that they offered coaching and I signed up. I insisted on their best coach, someone who also had children at home. Working with Kip dramatically changed my life. We began working with the habits: "begin with the end in mind" and "put first things first." He asked me to begin with a personal mission statement. He engaged my identity. Who has God made me to be? What is my purpose? He asked me to create a list he called my "clarified values in light of my relationships" and use it in a weekly planning process.*

> *— I am in a life-giving relationship with the Creator and Lover of all.*
>> *He transforms my life every day.*
>> *We abide in one another every day*
>> *He impacts the world through me every day.*
> *— I am the steward of my own capacity (I am daily renewing the foundation of a great life through self-care).*
>
> *— Michele and I are delighting in our awesome relationship!*
>
> *— We are delighting in our warm, close relationship with Mario and Luisa.*
>
> *— We love and treasure our extended and adopted family.*
>
> *— We love and treasure those we come in contact with at work.*
>
> *— We have a large, lasting impact on the world.*

I have a very large smile on my face and am eager to make all of these things true. I am buzzing with motivation. The fast track is definitely running.

In the first year of activating the fast track in this way I was the #2 sales representative in the country and took all seven weeks of vacation the same year. Something else interesting came out of this process. Up to this point I had been acting as if being the number one sales rep in my Fortune 500 company was my highest value. As you can see, it didn't even make the list. The paradox is that I continued to perform very well. The fast track allowed me to live from the depth of who I really am in a way that allowed me to be more while still performing at a high level.

Energy, motivation, and engagement are the output of a smoothly running fast track with a solid and joyful identity. Identity is the core function for the fast track. When identity is solid and fits with our values, families, work group, and mission, we find ourselves directing (leading) ourselves and our group in the same direction. *The ability to lead is learned and can be optimized.*

If we divide our interactions with others into a core purpose and skills, we find the skills are often called emotional intelligence (EQ) or emotional competence (both terms coined by Daniel Goleman[1]). The core purpose is to maintain and guide our identities as individuals and groups. But how does this fast-track guidance system actually work?

BREAKTHROUGHS IN "SEEING" THE BRAIN

Prior to the 1990s the brain could only be studied once it was dead. Brain function was studied by testing people with brain damage and then checking their brain once they died to see where the damage had been. X-rays helped with rough measurements but X-rays could not tell what the parts they photographed were actually doing. Well into the 1980s, external performance tests were still the way to check for brain function. If someone could not see color then the color center in the brain had problems. If someone could not move her right hand then the right-hand control center in the brain became a suspect. I (Jim) did these neurological tests for the neurosurgeons at the Veterans Administration hospital as part of my training. I was a sort of human brain scan machine.

As technology created computerized brain scans that could examine live brains without damage, science began to study living brains in action. For example, we could say what parts of the brain had to work for spiritual experiences to occur. Combining this new information with the old knowledge of pathways for processing allowed us to see where things got "stuck" on their way to proper function.

Dr. Alan Schore from UCLA, who has been called the "Einstein of psychiatry," was the key thinker in unifying many fields of study into a coherent model of the brain. The first of Schore's three-volume set on how the brain learns identity and motivation through joy contains over a hundred pages of references for those who would like a deeper look at the science.[2]

What emerged from the brain labs was a picture of an experience-processing pathway that started at the bottom of the right brain and worked its way forward, going through a series of four major steps.[3] On the way to the top, the brain compiles a picture of "where I am" in relation to the world at this moment. This relational picture is updated six times a second. In people with great resilience and capacity the process almost never became stuck. Other low-joy brains (ones with few relational competencies) became "cramped" in places and shut off in others and the picture of "where I am in the world" was not completed. The critical point between the brain functioning well or starting to fail is where it runs out of joy and begins to run on fear as its motivation. Incomplete fast-track processing is a form of being "out of touch" that makes us reactive, rigid with serious implications to living, and leading ineffectively.

> Throughout Scripture we see that joy is the motivator to enable us to endure suffering.

Joy is a renewable energy source that the brain is wired to prefer. Again—there is good news here for leaders. If your people are struggling with low morale, or you are fighting to keep your heart in the battle, brain science may offer some unexpected help.

Science is reminding us of the importance the Bible has placed on joy. Jesus said He came so that our joy might be complete.[4] The Psalms taught us that joy is found in the face of God.[5] The routine blessing of the high priest was that God's face might shine on us.[6] Throughout Scripture we see that joy is the motivator that enables us to endure suffering. Jesus endured the cross for the joy that was set before Him.[7] Persecution is to be met with joy.[8] Trials are to be met with joy.[9] Paul rejoiced in what he suffered for the Colossians.[10] He and Silas sang when they were in prison recovering from their wounds.[11] Scripture has a lot to say about joy and how it grows our capacity to deal with hardship. As Nehemiah wrote, "The joy of the Lord is your strength."[12]

The conclusion of this new science is that relational joy is the natural means for growing a strong, resilient mind. Joy is a natural and sustainable fuel for engagement and the most desirable and powerful of motivating factors in our lives over the long haul, as Jim Martini discovered for himself. (He is now the CEO and optimizing outreach at Life Model Works.) Building a group identity based on joy is the optimal path for leadership.

WHEN THE ELEVATOR BECOMES JAMMED

To understand the workings of the fast-track processing pathway, think of an elevator in a four-story building. What happens when the elevator becomes jammed between the second and third floors or cannot open the door on the fourth floor? People and goods don't get where they're going. Business slows down. When this happens in the brain, important parts of leadership and identity do not arrive on time or get diverted.

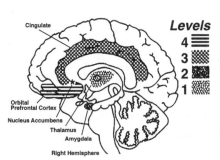

Most people know that the brain is separated into a left and right hemisphere. The right side of our brain dominates our core identity. The right side of the brain is largely nonverbal and operates much faster than the left side of our brain. This right-sided master system impacts our emotions and relationships faster than we have time to think about consciously. From bottom to top, the right brain is designed to seek, build, and thrive on joyful relationships. This design can be seen in the four sequential levels of brain function that moves from the base of the brain to the top.

Level one: The attachment center (*thalamus* and *nucleus accumbens*). This is the deepest part of the brain. It is the most basic thing about us. The attachment center lights up when we feel like being with someone. As I (Marcus) sit at a coffee shop and write this, I am with my twenty-four-year-old daughter. Her cell phone rang, and I watched her jump from her seat. "Oh my goodness! I can't believe it's you!" There was total joy on her face and in her voice as she greeted a friend from college. Seeing the name on her cell phone triggered her attachment center to light up at the expectation of a joyful connection with her friend.

The attachment center is all about relationships. Its greatest pleasure is joyful attachment. Its greatest pain is relational loss. Our deepest need and most desperate craving is joyful relationships. People will do crazy things in the pursuit of joyful relationship. They will leave the ministry, abandon their families, and run up their credit cards. The most common problems at level one are addictions. We ignore joy at our own peril.

Let us say you have seen a dog. When level one determines that some part of the world around us is personally meaningful to us (at this moment in time), that information is placed on the elevator and begins going floor by floor to the executives in the penthouse on the fourth floor. Level one determines that dogs are important to you and loads this dog on the elevator to move on to level two.

Level two: The assessment center (*amygdala*). Most people know level two for its fight-or-flight response. When the experience-processing elevator reaches the second floor the reality inside is inspected to see if this is good, bad, or scary. By consulting the library of memories for important good, bad, and scary moments the value of this moment's elevator cargo is determined. The library may say:

dogs bark loudly and lunge. Dog = scary. The library may say: dogs bite. Dog = bad. Or, the library may say: dogs love you when no one else does. Dogs = good. Level two does not reason or change its mind. Level two checks the library. The books in this library are there forever. In cases of post-traumatic stress (PTSD), the elevator sticks at the second floor. A national code-red emergency response is called and no more thinking will follow.

Leaders who get stuck operating out of their fight-or-flight response to life are going to have a hard time experiencing joy for themselves or creating joy in their environments. Once fear becomes the dominant motivator, nearly everything in life becomes a problem to be solved.

Level three: The attunement center *(cingulate cortex)*. Our sample dog is sent to the third floor wearing one or more of the good, bad, and scary labels, and here the elevator comes into the range where we can observe the contents directly. The third-floor door opens with the question, "Can anyone relate to this?" In this example, perhaps, "Do you see how cute this puppy is?" We are on the attunement floor where we can compare our responses with one other person at a time. Science calls this "mutual mind" and with it we bridge minds with others.

The third-floor processing department "reads" people and synchronizes with their feelings. When this skill is fully developed, we feel at peace. The third floor allows us to synchronize with God and find peace by perceiving His perspective on life. When our thoughts get in sync with God's thoughts, we feel a sense of shalom. This is what the apostle Paul meant in Colossians 3:15 when he wrote, "Let the peace of Christ rule in your hearts."

I (Marcus) look at it this way: When my mind is racing with anxious thoughts and I am sorting through all of them looking for God, I can know that I have found Him when I find those thoughts that bring me peace. This doesn't mean that I have heard the voice of God. It means that I am getting my thoughts in sync with His.

The third floor does have the brain's connections to awareness of God, but it also connects us to other people so we really "get" what is going on around us relationally. When level three is working we never feel isolated. With defects in the construction and training on the third floor, people become awkward socially and misread people on a regular basis. They "see" things that simply aren't there. Learning to synchronize with people and attune to their feelings is an important relational skill. Without this skill, we will feel isolated even in a crowd.

With the question answered of how someone else would see our reality, the elevator now goes to the penthouse for the executive decisions about how I will act under these conditions.

Level four: The identity center (*prefrontal cortex*). This is where my people's core values help me guide my life, attend to what matters and act like my joyful, relational self. Once my identity-based response is clear, the fast track is finished and the experience is passed down to conscious, slow-track management for implementation.

This fourth level represents the highest level of brain function. Our identity finds its capacity to stay in charge and grows with the experience of relational joy. Every time people are glad to be together and withstand adversity, their joy-strength grows and their emotional capacity becomes greater.

The fast-track elevator has now taken us to the top floor of the right brain. We are about 160 milliseconds (or one-sixth of a second) into this experience. By now we know we would like to pet the doggie and send the order over to management slow-track to find out if the owner will allow us to pet her dog. That process will take much longer. Management does not yet know we have seen a dog but they will discover that in about 40 more milliseconds when conscious thought completes its first dog picture.

The RARE habits we explore in this book link all four levels of the right brain together. These four levels require training to work together and make the human brain a relational machine that runs on joy. When everything is operating the way it is supposed to, the brain runs smoothly. We feel like ourselves. We function with low stress and high joy. However, when this process breaks down, our brain starts to malfunction. Instead of high joy and low stress, we start living out of fear and the problems of life take center stage, overwhelming our relational capacity.

BORN PREDATORY

Unlike computers, the brain must self-assemble as it grows. It must seek what it needs and feed itself. We do not have to teach babies to be hungry. The desire to feed ourselves is in the wiring. When we are born, the world is there to eat. Even mommy is there to eat. Everything goes into baby's mouth. The problem to solve is how to get what I want to eat and the brain tries to find the easiest solution. This is the basis for our "predatory" response. Everyone is born predatory. We do not have to learn to be predatory.

THE FOUR LEVELS GROW AND DEVELOP
ONE FLOOR AT A TIME

We are born without the third floor completed and the fourth floor yet to be built. Most of the major growth of the right brain is finished by eighteen months of age. The implication of this process is that the brain must be trained as it is grown. Building the executive penthouse where leadership and identity rule depends on building a strong and functional third floor below. Construction is on a strict time schedule and many times the fourth floor goes up with major problems on the floor below. It should be no surprise then that most of the trouble we see comes from defects on the third floor (where we learn to sync relationally) that was built in the six months after birth—whether or not that was a good time for building emotional competence into the fast track.

TRAINED TO BE PROTECTIVE

As we grow we need to learn that everything is not there for us to eat right now. In other words, we realize that many of the best resources for maintaining our identity must be saved and not used as soon as we figure out how to get them. Here come the skills of emotional competence. Protecting what we value is the role of maturity and the function of the last part of the brain to develop. We call this penthouse on the fourth floor the right, orbital, prefrontal cortex. Its purpose is a joyful identity for us and our people. Here is the office where RARE leadership is grown and trained.

Protector responses are all learned. Protector responses are much more sophisticated than the simple and fast predator moves. In one sense it can be said that leadership is entirely about dealing with weakness by anticipating, preventing, repairing, and strengthening the effects of weakness. Market opportunities, team building, motivation, and training all depend upon a leader's response to weakness.

What often happens is that the fast track of the brain is responding like an untrained predator would, while the slow track is trying to control the reactions and act like a professional or a Christian or a parent. While this seems like the best anyone can do given the slow thinking on the reasoning side of the brain, a whole different world opens up if we can actually *train* the fast track to be protective rather than predatory. *We propose that this training is not only possible but is what makes a good leader.*

Because predator thinking is wired into the brain, it never goes away. Many Christians have fought a pointless and losing fight trying to eliminate impulsive sexual thoughts, reactions, urges, and calculations. We are wired to know how to exploit others. Babies, beasts, and bishops all know how to exploit weakness!

The actual solution is not trying to suppress predatory thoughts but to find a better response to weakness. It is clear that those who protect others must be as good at spotting weakness as any predator. What is needed is a strong sense of how I and my kind of people respond to the naked, poor, lost, confused, and otherwise vulnerable people we see.

WHEN FEAR TAKES OVER

Every time the fast track runs out of relational joy the elevator becomes stuck at the third floor. When no one wants to understand or join our experience we become afraid. The brain only knows two ways to generate motivational fuel—a joy bond or a fear bond. We call this a "bond" because the exchange of joy or fear becomes our way of doing business with others.

When I have a joy bond with someone, I look forward to seeing them. Being with them brings joy and just thinking about being with them brings joy. However, when the second floor assessment center gets the message that the person I am bonded to is bad or scary, fear takes over instead of joy. I am not going to be free to act like myself. Instead, I am going to have to wear a carefully crafted mask that makes me look the way I need to look in order to get what I want out of the relationship.

When I function in joy, I operate out of the top two floors near the front of my brain. When I function in fear, I operate out of the second floor near the bottom and back of my brain. The back of the brain is not a good place to be. When the elevator is stuck between the second and third floor we are:

- nonrelational
- fixated on problems
- waiting for people and/or problems to go away
- unable to imagine relational solutions for problems
- feeling isolated and alone (it is all up to me)
- experiencing negative emotions more intensely

When operating out of the back of our brain due to fear we are often not aware that we are afraid in any way. We regularly see ourselves as self-sufficient. However, our thinking is actually locked on to negative consequences and how to stop them.

What happens if I don't (do the task I'm supposed to)?

- I'll lose my job
- The boss will get angry
- The board will not be happy
- My wife will kill me

These motives are so universally felt as to go unnoticed in most groups. In fact, leaders with poor right-brain skills will frequently rely on "what will happen if you don't" thinking for motivation, solving problems, and getting action.

We are not suggesting that leaders simply do whatever makes them happy: quite the opposite! We suggest that when fear becomes the dominant motivation in any group, that group will become toxic. When fear is the primary motivation for a leader, that leader will burn out and spread dysfunction to his group in the process. The point is how we solve problems. Will we solve them relationally, creatively, as a group, and with the best part of ourselves engaged in what we're doing? Or, will we solve problems in isolation, avoiding shame and any perception of failure, while hiding behind a mask that makes us look stronger than we really are?

HOW ISOLATION HURTS THE FAST TRACK

Anselm learned to drive without a car. He lived in a country where he saw cars but his family did not have one. Anselm learned to drive from video games where the faster you went the better and where crashes meant you just start over. As soon as he arrived in the US, Anselm got a license and a car . . . plus over $10,000 in fines the first year. We need a car to learn to drive a car. We need a piano to learn to play. We need engagement to learn engagement.

As we all hope Anselm will discover, the effect of a crash in real life does not necessarily guarantee a lesson learned. We need to anticipate things that might go wrong and learn to recover when they do go wrong. Both foreseeing and recovering are the work of the fast-track master system. And we learn these things when we are engaged, not isolated.

Here is the maxim: *A fast-track system produces isolation to the degree it was trained in isolation.*

What may throw us off is that people who are isolated in their heads may all be sitting in cubicles next to each other, packed in like sardines. How we detect isolation most clearly is in the joy levels of a group. The higher the joy level (glad to be together) when people engage group tasks, the lower the isolation level is in that group. When people must gather by the water cooler and away from the group tasks to find joy, then isolation is running their fast tracks. They are not recovering from crashes and returning to joy. Most commonly this leads to management rules rather than improved fast-track solutions. Our internal reactions will let us know our own competence. If our reaction is "let me listen to them and I bet I will have happy workers again" our competence is high and our fast track will want to overcome the workers' isolation. If our own fast track cramps up we will immediately head toward irritation and ways to manage such wasted time. We will need to find someone who can coach us on better relational engagement without neglecting improved management.

A RARE AND WONDERFUL LIFE

By this point you might be understanding your own "fast track" a little better. The good news is, habits that make for a RARE and wonderful life can be learned. We can live our lives and guide others with character, meaning, and purpose.

In our next chapter we will look at some indicators that our fast-track system might need repairs. In the meantime, here are some things you can do to test your own fast track.

Brain Science for RARE Leadership

Testing our fast-track function

We can quickly lose fast-track function. The executive control center of the brain (PFC) can nod off from fatigue, stress, depression, or just feeling overwhelmed. It can pass out from drugs. Many factors can leave the "front office" unoccupied during business hours. Because the brain is quite fast we can even "slam the door" almost instantly when we see someone who upsets us or hear about a problem we dread.

Unless we have ways to test for fast-track operation we will not consciously know when we have lost our leader. As mentioned at the start of this chapter, brain scans show us what is running, but due to expense and machine size this solution is not one we can take with us to work. If you remember, I (Jim) was a human "brain scan machine" before machines were invented. The older method used the unique functions of different brain systems to test their operation. Because every part of the brain has specific functions, we can test for those functions. Showing someone an image will test the brain's visual centers, for example. The many exclusive functions of the executive prefrontal cortex provide many possible tests. Here are a few that are simple to observe.

- *Curiosity*—Am I really interested in what others are thinking, or am I rehearsing my options?
- *Relationship is bigger than the problem*—Am I thinking how this event will bring out the strengths in our relationship, or is my focus on how to solve the problem (or just make it stop, which is even more primitive thinking)?
- *We do not feel alone*—We remember the people who would be at our side even when they are not available and are encouraged by who they would remind us we are.
- *Appreciation*—We can enjoy "smelling the roses" and savoring the simple pleasures of life.
- *Shalom*—A sense of calm underlies our distress; we are confident that we will know (or discover) how to handle this situation well, providing what has been called a "non-anxious presence."

The better trained and stronger our executive brain has become the more we can keep the executive functions working well during time of stress, problems, and upset. We will consider how to build and strengthen our executive center later in this book. Begin by building a sense of appreciation you can sustain for five minutes at a time.

DISCUSSION QUESTIONS

1. Was there a particular story in this chapter that resonated with you? Why?

2. Why is fast-track training important for leaders? What are the negative consequences of ignoring such training? What are the positive benefits of training it well?

3. In this chapter the fast-track system is described as a four-story elevator that is only partially constructed at birth. You can think of fast-track training as completing the work on this elevator system that never got finished. This can require repairs (healing) or new construction (growth). Are you aware of areas in your own life where repair is needed?

4. What are some of the signs that joy has broken down in a community?

5. What is the difference between managing a group through a lack of joy and leading a group through a lack of joy?

CHAPTER 4

When the Fast Track Needs Fixing

The cost of toxic community

A LARGE POSTER of Dietrich Bonhoeffer and Martin Luther King Jr. hung on the wall facing the entrance to the main office. Inside was a German community dedicated to the recovery of those who were nearly destroyed by the Nazi machine. Thomas Gerlach helped lead the community. He had lived in Israel and worked on a kibbutz, and spent most of his adult life dedicated to building a Bonhoeffer-like Christian community. He was more than familiar with the cost of discipleship.

The poster of Bonhoeffer silently pointed to a deeper injury for Thomas and his family. Thomas's grandfather was the SS officer who had hunted down and imprisoned Bonhoeffer. In an amazing story of redemption, first the officer's son and then Thomas had discovered and been transformed by Bonhoeffer's writings.

The cost of discipleship started with the price of being disowned. Determined to make amends for their family's role, Thomas and his father dedicated their lives to both building a Bonhoeffer-inspired community and undoing as many of the officer's evil deeds as possible. To this end they spent their lives and resources on helping those who had survived. By building a community in their home they provided a place where some of the most emotionally damaged survivors might learn to live and work again. Standing at the door and looking at the poster of Bonhoeffer was silently mind-bending.

It is hard to conceive of a family that became more relationally invested in leadership. Every day was a shared life. Family was both natural and spiritual. Weak and strong lived together. Tender responses to weak members were to rule their lives. Prayer, resolving strongholds, and strict adherence to Bible study for all guidance were absolutes for life. Life was very hard but faced resolutely.

People in the group who wanted to be loved by God were despised.

Yet something was not going as it should. With every aspect of life carefully managed, the joy levels did not improve and over many years everyone became more and more tired.

What was invisible to everyone was that their fast-track fuel had not changed. When I (Jim) visited this community, I found people speaking a great deal about God—but unaware that much of what drove them day-to-day was avoiding anger from leaders and each other. While any verbal outbursts were rare, no one in the community knew how to return to joy from anger. As a result, someone had to get angry (or threaten to) any time results were badly needed. Some community members were as regular as a calendar with their outbreaks while others became angry under pressure.

Community leaders needed to have the strongest anger to keep the group on track. Most often the threat was that God would become angry. God kept control without joy, and people who wanted to be loved by God were despised.

Leadership conflicts developed around the nature of God and their group identity. As Thomas struggled with anger, frustration, anxiety, disappointment about promised healing, and fear of abandonment, his identity began to crack. His desire to talk about God's love and joy was labeled as a spiritual attack on the community.

Eventually this dispute over identity broke the community. Thomas says:

I was changed even against my will before I could make changes. My personal breakdown after seeing all my hopes end, my beloved wife dying and my ministry failing left me helpless. I could no longer run my life or even lead myself. In that moment as I was looking for comfort and strength, the word of God showed me that giving up all control is freedom. God takes control as I give up control. I embraced servant leadership while feeling the urgent push to separate myself from an abusive context.

Leaving spiritual abuse behind left me at a crossroad. Do I regain control of my life again as fast as I can to quench that feeling of insecurity or go in the opposite direction by embracing my insecurity and helplessness while leaving control to God? Choosing to give up control began a process of dying like Paul describes in Romans. However, the motivation of change came from joy and freedom even in a breakdown.

The freedom I experience is the most valuable thing I have. Freedom has to be protected and tended, as it can be lost very quickly. I am once again a pastor, this time of a small Church with a long tradition. I have entered a position with power to control others and so lose my freedom along with theirs. As I have grown in understanding of being a servant, my motivation comes more from what I am and how I feel in this moment than from what I am doing or achieving. This sets me free, especially when I am preaching. I talk to God and myself while others listen. The congregation likes it—that is joy in operation!

When I am there and I can rejoice in being close to God and those I love, work is easy, leadership is motivating others, and fellowship is good even with very difficult people.

Leaders with fast-track problems will use whatever emotions block their personal return to joy to create motivation in themselves and others.

HOW AVOIDING NEGATIVE EMOTIONS TURNS TOXIC

One of the elders at my (Jim's) church depended on the negative feelings of shame to motivate action. He wanted me to take some work off his hands and began working on stirring guilt and shame in me. He pointed out how "good Christians" would do the work he had in mind for me. The more I said no, the angrier he got. After about ten minutes he exploded, "You just refuse to feel guilty, don't you!" This time I said yes.

When leaders begin to be swayed by who is going to get upset, they are surrendering their guidance to the most emotionally unstable person in their group.

We often use avoiding unpleasant emotions as a way to motivate ourselves. Procrastination is a motivation pattern generated by avoiding the most impending negative outcome. Only when the project reaches the "failure is imminent" level does work get completed. In the long term, motivation through avoiding bad feelings is hard to sustain. Instead of staying on track (like completing my work) I will look for other ways to feel better (like drinking some coffee and having just one more of those brownies).

Most people depend on avoiding unpleasant feelings for motivation by reminding themselves and others of what might happen:

- That is going to upset so-and-so!
- Don't make me mad!
- What if he finds out?
- I am going to put on weight.
- If I don't, then . . .

When leaders begin to be swayed by who is going to get upset, they are surrendering their guidance to the most emotionally unstable person in their group. When leaders must revert to raising their voices and inciting fear or upset in their group, they are using toxic motivation to motivate others through avoidance.

As unpleasant as the "big six" negative emotions of anger, fear, sadness, shame, disgust, and hopeless despair can be, they do not need to block us from relationships. It is only when emotions block the way to relationship that using emotions for motivation becomes toxic. The elder who tried to motivate me through shame expected that shame would block me from relationships and that I would work very hard to avoid the pain. Since I could feel shame *and* maintain relationships with people who were not glad to be with me, the motivation didn't work.

Here is where things turned toxic. Now the leader had to find other ways to block me from relationships in order to get his way. I had to be eliminated from the group as the elder needed to be surrounded by people who would work to avoid shame. Does this toxic pattern sound familiar?

WARNING SIGNS

How are we to spot when fast-track training is needed since, as we have seen, the "managerial" slow track cannot really watch what the fast track is doing? Several patterns emerge when the slow track is running without guidance.

Increasing isolation—characterized by such attitudes as "I'd rather do it myself!" or "I alone am left to do the work." People are managed and leaders stay aloof without forming any friendships in their group. Rather than seeking the shelter of each other, members avoid the isolation of rejection and criticism.

Increasing attention given to motivation by warning of negative outcomes. "If you don't do this, such-and-such will happen." Something might show up on our performance review. Or the person wanting results becomes angry or threatening.

The sense that others will not listen unless I make things worse is a strong hint that our fast track has shut down and relational solutions are giving way to "management by avoiding negative experiences." Weaknesses in others (or ourselves) become the problem that is keeping us from good results.

Going predatory happens when weaknesses are criticized, power advantages are exploited, and people look out for "number one."

So what do we do?

Healing opens the way for building a better elevator with good relational (fast-track) habits. Healing does not suddenly provide habits that were never learned.

A full catalog of damages and repairs to the fast track is far beyond the scope of this book. But we need to determine whether the need is to train our fast track—or heal a damaged system.

Two experiences may help us understand.

HEALING AN ANGRY MAN

My (Marcus's) father taught at Trinity Evangelical Divinity School and met with a lot of future leaders there. One of his students was a handsome, articulate, kind young man with a pretty wife and two young children. He was the sort of graduate churches love to hire. Everything looked picture-perfect on the outside. One Saturday morning, however, my dad got a call from this student asking if he could come see him. The student had flown into a rage, thrown a phone across the room, and scared his kids to death. His wife had given him an ultimatum, as this wasn't the first time something like this had happened.

During their meeting that morning, my father also discovered that the young man had a hidden pornography addiction. Thankfully, my father was able to help this man resolve the strongholds in his life and find healing for some early childhood trauma. As a result he was able to save his marriage and function successfully in ministry for many years. This soon-to-be-graduate was the sort of person who would interview really well. Any church would have been happy to have him. But without some sort of assessment in place he might well have entered ministry leadership as a ticking time bomb.

> People from low-joy environments seem more drawn to religious causes.

LEARNING NEW HABITS IN THE NORTH COUNTRY

The first snow arrived at the North Country about the same time as I (Jim) reached the area. Martha was part of inviting me to visit their community. In return I would teach a bit about joy.

Martha had been part of various communities where she observed that too much leadership emphasized power, not relationship. At this community, much of the group life revolved around "re-habiting" themselves from the patterns that they learned growing up. This included their leadership methods.

The community was aware that many members arrived in a wounded state. These wounds often produced intense emotional reactions to the strains of community life and service under a vow of poverty. Martha recognized that people from low-joy backgrounds seem more drawn to religious causes and that their wounded ways often contributed to lowering the joy in the community. The directors were concerned that their mission leaders around the world were finding that the strain went beyond their capacities in the field. On top of full-time mission work, those who ran the local houses were trying to help their wounded members live in mature, relational ways so as to fulfill the duty of the moment. This load was frequently too much for local leaders.

There is much more to the story. But for our purposes, I will just say that the leader of the community, an Irishman I'll call Pat, was at first suspicious of me and what I was doing there. But as I listened to him I admired his willingness to speak up, his discernment of the problem, and his desire to protect his flock. In minutes he and I were fast friends thanks to a sufficient supply of fast-track skills that enabled me to act like myself in the situation and remain relational.

Here is the problem: Without healing, the brain often cannot be trained. Without training, the brain often cannot recover. Healing opens the way for building a better "elevator" with good relational habits.

Martha concludes, "It is crucial that the leader live a joy- and shalom-based life if there is to be joy and peace in the community. Problems are inevitable and maturity levels will always be variable. But given a good model of leadership I think the community can thrive and grow."

WHY TRAINING THE FAST TRACK IS CRUCIAL
TO LEADERSHIP SUCCESS

The right hemisphere of the brain is the nonverbal side where our deepest feelings reside and our attachments are formed. It doesn't matter whether we're talking about an attachment to a puppy, a piece of cake, a shot of whiskey, an abusive uncle, or our newborn baby— all attachments are formed in the fast-track system. A well-trained fast track operates in a protective, life-giving way to the attachments it forms. A poorly trained master system will tend to be predatory, defensive, fear-bound, and selfish.

After this quick review of some effects from an incompletely trained fast track, it should be clear that people whom we must lead often flood with unpleasant emotions, operate in isolation, react unthinkingly, and take advantage of others. Leaders do not simply need to have overcome these issues in themselves but must help their group overcome these factors—*even before leading becomes possible.*

THIS IS YOUR BRAIN ON FEAR

A final word about the danger of isolation. The untrained fast track operates in isolation—which is directly related to fear. The brain fears any situations that will "leave me on my own." Anything that leads to abandonment, rejection, lack of help, or overwhelming emotions becomes something to avoid. Instead of knowing we have other people we can call on, instead of remembering "how it is like me and my people to act" (as the best God created us), we are left to solve our problems on our own.

Here is the nexus of most leadership problems. *The hardest times to lead are precisely those times when each group member feels "on his or her own" and isolated.* Everyone just wants to make the problem go away and just . . . stop.

The disadvantages of operating in fear mode are far too extensive to even consider here. We must mention, however, that fear mode does NOT send a notice to our conscious brain that isolation thinking has now taken over, thus leaving the slow-track without guidance and with no warning. If the slow-track notices anything at all, it is explained as "I like to take care of this myself."

In the next chapter we will look at the difference between the way immature leaders look at their task and emotionally mature leaders look at their task. In the process we will reveal the surprising key to vibrant leadership.

Brain Science for RARE Leadership

The management assistant runs the left-brain slow track

The brain's executive is in the penthouse (right prefrontal cortex) but that is not where a healthy brain uses most of its energy. A healthy fast-track system does not do most of the brain's work. As long as we are acting like our true, joyful, and relational selves, the executive watches and learns. We should remember that the master system tracks our identity by running faster than conscious thought. We never have to stop and wonder, "Now who was I?" Our identity, who we are, always seems obvious *before* we even look at what is going on around us (except in a very damaged brain).

The hard work of managing life around us is done in the assistant director's office in the left prefrontal cortex. The management assistant burns much of the energy it takes to run the brain. For many years this high-energy consumption fooled scientists into thinking that the left-sided assistant was in charge.

Our hard-working slow-track assistant manages our life at the speed of consciousness. We are consciously aware of whatever thinking and work is being done in the left prefrontal management offices. We are aware as our plans and operations are laid out. Our manager works with tools such as concepts, plans, agreements, contracts, rules, problem identification, problem solving, and choices. Provided these plans are consistent with our identities, the fast-track executive in the right side penthouse is content to watch.

But it is a huge mistake to believe that the slower conscious activity we can watch is more important than the faster identity activity we cannot watch directly. While conscious speed activity does solve problems, it does not ensure that the most important problems are solved, that problems are solved the least harmful way, or that our organization remains together and on track. We need think no further than church fights, church splits, and an organization's loss of a sense of its mission to see the damage a focus on "problems" can cause.

It is rare that the slow-track management even notices if the fast-track executive identity is "out of the office." Even the symptoms that our fast track is down generally go unnoticed: operations have lost all sense of whom we value; we do not sense we may be part of the problem; and problems seem bigger than relationships. Yet our management system plows ahead consciously, trying to become whatever will yield results and seeing anyone who disagrees with us as the problem.

When operating alone, the slow-track manager simply explains, blames, or solves the problems using whatever makes sense to him or her at the moment. What "makes sense" is observably strange thinking to external observers. When that slow track is running unsupervised in a leader's head, people around can see that the leader obviously believes his or her own explanations, but group members will not see things the same way. The leader's relational circuits will be off.

In our next segment we will examine what generally knocks out the executive fast track and how to wake up the "boss." More importantly, we will examine how to build a stronger fast-track executive who grows and develops a sophisticated and capable group identity.

DISCUSSION QUESTIONS

1. Which elements of Thomas Gerlach's story were most inspirational to you? What lessons about leadership came through most clearly?

2. Have you been in an environment where a particular negative emotion of the "big six" seemed to be necessary for the leader to motivate people to action? What was the emotion and how did it impact your experience?

3. Which negative emotion do you turn to most often to motivate you to get things done? Which one do you use to motivate others?

4. How would you summarize the dangers of an undeveloped fast track to a leader? To his community?

CHAPTER 5

Don't Take Your Eye Off the Fast Track

When you know who you are, you get results

WITH ONLY ONE shot to go, the American sharpshooter looked poised to win his second gold medal of the 2004 Olympic Games. He had never scored below a 9.3 in any of his prior rounds, and only needed the relatively mediocre score of 7.2 to clinch the prize. He took his time, lined up his shot, breathed slowly, squeezed the trigger calmly and watched as the bullet ripped through the target in a perfect bull's-eye. He had done it! He leapt to his feet and began to celebrate the shot of a lifetime!

Jubilation, however, was short-lived. As it turned out, he had made a perfect shot, but at the wrong target. The result was a score of zero, an eighth place finish, and a lot of heartache.

In leadership there are two primary targets from which we need to choose. Target #2 is by far the most popular and may even seem non-negotiable. That #2 target is "getting results." When hitting our numbers is our primary target, we focus on things like making a profit, winning games, expanding our market, and growing our ministry. For many of us, such a focus seems so self-evident that we never even consider that there might be an alternative. We contend that leaders must keep target #2 as *second* priority and aim first at target #1: building group identity. The prime target for leadership is the culture of our organization. It answers the questions, "Who are we?" and "How is it like us to act?"

Target 1: Identity	Target 2: Results
Leadership	Management
Fast-track	Slow-track
If Placed First	**If Placed First**
Joy-based	*Fear-based*
High motivation	*Low motivation*
High bonding	*Low bonding*
High sacrifice	*Low sacrifice*

Results are the slow-moving target that catches our conscious attention. Our slow-track, conscious thinking takes aim at the obvious and moves toward management solutions. RARE leaders have discovered that everything in our brain (and in the minds that serve under us) powers up when we aim for a powerful group identity first. When we know who we are, we get our kind of results.

The Marines come to mind as a classic example of a group that wants results but focuses on group identity. The Marines don't necessarily win every battle they fight. But they act like Marines in every situation they face. Sometimes victory isn't really an option. However, success isn't always defined by victory. It is found in fighting like Marines no matter what the outcome may be.

A friend of mine (Marcus) told me about a sports psychology group that ran an interesting experiment. They took a group of Marines and a group of professional athletes and ran them through the same drill. On the surface it seemed like a simple assignment. They were to run across an open field, touch a fence, and run back as fast as they could. The wrinkle in this little experiment was that the event took place in Florida and there was a small body of water beside the field. The people running the exercise had arranged for a fake alligator to be put in the water. When they gave the signal, it would come up out of the water. The point of the experiment was to see the difference in how the two groups responded.

The first to go were the professional athletes. They took off with the speed you would expect of athletes trained to compete. However, as soon as the alligator lunged out of the water, the race came to an abrupt end and they all scattered as quickly as they could. No one finished the race.

When the Marines showed up, they had no idea of what awaited them or of what had happened to the athletes. They simply toed the line and took off as soon as the whistle blew. Halfway to the wall, the alligator came surging out of the water. Their reaction was immediate and universal. They all stopped, faced the alligator, and started to laugh. They all finished the race.

The difference between the two groups was that one had been trained to endure hardship and face potential threats. The other had merely been trained to compete. In the same way, many leaders understand competition. They want better results than their competitors. But this is not the same thing as knowing how to endure hardship.

John Maxwell tells the story of Morgan Wooten, a remarkable high school basketball coach who set all sorts of records for winning. (His career record was 1274-192).[1] He got consistently winning results. However, a closer look at his program will tell you that results were not his primary target. His target was a culture of transformation. It was not uncommon for Wooten to have one of his players living with his family. Unlike coaches who use their players to build their programs, he used his program to change the lives of his players.

> Leaders with high emotional maturity will always be community builders.

DUNGY: "LET'S JUST DO WHAT WE DO"

Understanding that a strong group identity should be our primary target establishes a benchmark that helps us evaluate where we are as an organization. Motivated by joy, the group understands that excellence is just part of being who they are and what they do. However, when we make results our primary target, we create a fear-based motivation for our performance. The result is a toxic environment characterized by low motivation, low bonding, and low excellence with little reason to sacrifice for the greater good.

Leaders with high emotional maturity will always be community builders. RARE leaders call out what is best in people and remind them how to act like themselves when problems become a serious challenge.

I (Marcus) lived in Indianapolis when Tony Dungy was the coach of the Colts. In the media he would often say things like, "We just need to do what we do, and we'll be okay." I really liked that expression: "Let's just do what we do." He didn't say, "Let's just win, baby!" He didn't say, "We're going to do whatever it takes to win." He said, "We're going to strive to be the best version of ourselves we can be, and trust that if we do that, we're going to win more than we lose." It apparently worked, because during his tenure the Colts were the winningest team in the NFL.

> Groups with a healthy identity shine brightest in times of trouble.

WAYNE GORDON AND HIS PEOPLE

A group's identity is formed by the answers to two simple questions: "Who are my people?" and "How is it like us to act?" We see this in high school all the time. Teens create an identity for themselves based on who they hang out with. If a teenager sees herself as part of the popular crowd, she knows who she is and what the expected behavior is for her group. If she is part of the Goth crowd, she will have a different identity with different expectations about how her people act, but her identity is still formed by the group.

Not all group identities are healthy. Terrorists, gang members, and cults have some of the strongest group identities of anyone in the world as we saw in chapter 2. Leaders build a group identity in which people fear and even hate those on the outside. The power of a group identity is harnessed for destructive goals.

A healthy group identity is characterized by joy. People like belonging to the group. Team members look forward to being together. Members know that no matter what problems arise, the group will face them together. Individuals aren't going to be left alone in their distress. In fact, groups with a healthy identity shine brightest in times of trouble. There is never any question that they are in this together and no one is going to be left behind.

At least four books have been written about Wayne ("Coach") Gordon's life experiences. I (Jim) visited his church in the Lawndale area of Chicago. Coach has been a pastor in this high-crime community for forty years. With a hint of sad irony, I say that Coach has an easy time avoiding target #2 (managed results) where he lives because his situation is unmanageable. Coach could not keep people from breaking into his house, he could not keep neighbors from being killed, he could not stop people from selling drugs, he could not prevent police from cracking people's heads, he could not keep youth out of jails.

But the team of addiction counselors, lawyers, teachers, tutors, pastors, job trainers, cooks, medical personnel, and staff working with Coach tells us quite clearly that Coach is after results. His books *Leadership Revolution, Who Is My Neighbor,* and *Real Hope for Chicago* back up what a day with Coach reveals: Coach is about building leaders through relationships. Coach's leaders are the people of his neighborhood. His tool is the formation of a solid Christian identity that will withstand the pressures all around their homes and church. Every leader is someone with a story of a changed identity. As a group, they not only reflect this identity to each other but they step into the street to find a new identity in the people who least believe transformation is possible.

Coach Gordon and the visionary civil rights leader John Perkins have taken their transforming, relational leadership development to the inner cities of America and the world through the Christian Community Development Association (CCDA). Coach is now working with the Life Model (the foundation for this book) to improve the effectiveness of his leadership training. By knowing how joy transforms the fast-track, he hopes to build better leaders for the inner city and even higher joy in his cute little granddaughter. Coach is a RARE leader.

KIM: "ENGAGING ON A HEARTFELT LEVEL"

Kim Specker is a life transformation coach for leaders and professionals. Kim is the lead coach for an award-winning healthcare organization. Previously she operated a small-business consulting firm after moving from a position as division controller for a Fortune 500 company. Expertise in career management and recruitment and client relations experience all give us a hint that Kim has emotional competence and management expertise.

Kim is not an either/or leader when it comes to fast and slow tracks. Kim has learned where to keep her eyes focused. Notice how skilled management follows Kim around as she attends to relationships.

> *I was motivated to make changes in my leadership style because I realized that if I were to have a team that would help me reach my goals and aspirations, I was going to have to help them reach theirs. I had to make the shift in engaging with my team at a heartfelt level rather than results-based outcomes. Also, [in] learning about their passions and discovering their life purpose.*
>
> *Currently in the role I am in, my success is measured on evidence-based outcomes. There is more and more willingness to recognize that my contributions to the organization go beyond the specific deliverables I am held accountable to provide. My relational and emotional maturity brings a sense of joy and peace to the team. My relational connections and the ability to stabilize the group when tension is present are recognized as attributes I bring to the leadership table.*

Reaching this stable and RARE fast-track leadership required some specific changes for Kim. She credits the Life Model with clarifying where she directs her attention.

> *I was motivated to make changes in my life because my lack of patience and intolerance for those who didn't respond like I wanted them to created tension, agitation and disappointment for me. I continually seemed to be living in a state of frustration;*

my expectations for others were greater than what they had for themselves. Sometimes I asked myself when life was going to get better. I was tired of living in frustration, disappointment, and never feeling satisfied. I wanted to be able to say that I truly enjoyed life and the people around me.

[My desire was that] people would want to be on my team because I had the reputation for having their best interest at heart. It is my hope that the best talent will want to be on my team whether it would be in the marketplace or in a volunteer role.

MARYELLEN AND BILL: "CULTIVATING RELATIONAL MATURITY"

Dr. Bill St. Cyr made his own study of brain science and healing and came to many of the same conclusions as the Life Model. While Bill developed ways of healing in community, his soon-to-be-wife Maryellen was searching the history of education for alternatives to the semi-toxic learning environment in most schools, even Christian institutions. She found a teaching model in the work of British educator Charlotte Mason, who combined a deep commitment to Christ with an astute understanding of child formation. When Maryellen and Bill encountered each other it was like the old commercials where chocolate crashes into peanut butter and they discover they go great together. The St. Cyrs envisioned Ambleside Schools International and began developing a high-joy, brain-friendly, and uniquely Christian school system.

The mission of Ambleside Schools International is to provide a "living" education that empowers students to author lives that are full and free, rich in relationship to God, self, others, ideas, work, and creation. It puts a primacy on formation and not mere information, on maximizing whole-person growth rather than short-term performance, providing the tools necessary to live well in all aspects of life, spiritual and intellectual, personal and professional, present and future. In a word, our goal is to cultivate maturity, the kind of maturity that makes for strong, healthy, joyful workers, spouses, parents, and followers of Christ.

. . . Imagine the fourteen-year-old who manages emotional distress well and stays on task when head and hand are tired; is clear about his/her responsibilities, doing his/her duty to the best of his/her ability; is relationally attuned, working well with teacher and classmates; is curious, asking many questions seeking knowledge in many fields of study; is careful, neat and accurate. Then, ask how well will such a student do in high school, in college, in life? The answer is clear . . .

In their efforts, however, the St. Cyrs encountered problem areas that represent the challenge to all leaders who want to create a RARE community:

Child learning level—the people we intend to benefit

Teacher level—the workers we train to lead and manage constituents

Administration level—the management we train to lead our workers

Parent level—the community that shapes our constituents

Board and community level—interface with the non-relational legal structures

Cultural level—relational rules and trends in the world

Personal level—on the seventh day we shall rest and be glad for home and work alike

Child: Children thrive when provided an optimal atmosphere, inspirational ideas, and joyful support in developing needed relational and academic maturity skills. This is true of all children, including those who struggle to focus attention, build relationships, and learn joyfully. Thus, children proved to be the easiest place to make their model work.

Teacher: Building joyful learners is work for a lifetime but the Ambleside's founders must also retrain the fast-track identity of every teacher so that they stay relational on the worst days and with the hardest students. Bill says:

*Thus, we have come to realize that an Ambleside class will not
rise higher than the emotional-relational maturity of its teacher
and an Ambleside school will not rise higher than the emotional-
relational maturity of its principal. These ideas cast a very
different vision for the responsibilities and needed skill of school
leadership.*

Administration: Administrators are expected to run schools in a
manner that conforms to legal requirements, organizes for impersonal
efficiency, and sets performance objectives that are totally non-
relational. Most schools hire administrators to achieve such management results. When almost every matrix and rule is a slow track,
the non-relational management tasks easily become the main target.

*At an Ambleside school, the job description of a head of school is
redefined. While efficient management of resources is essential, it
is secondary to maintaining an optimal school atmosphere and
ensuring teachers and students are thriving. Management must
serve mission and the mission is maturity. Persons cannot be
managed into maturity.*

Parent: Parents come with all levels of maturity and potential
strengths. Parents also have weaknesses in their fast tracks they have
passed to their children. Parents who run their identity on fear often
expect the school should run on fear but obtain better results. Upset
customers can be draining. Bill adds his observations about the expectations parents bring.

*As a network of private Christian schools, we are entrusted by
parents with their two most precious possessions, their children
and their money. They continue to entrust us with the education
of their children so long as the children appear to be flourishing
and parental experience of the school is high joy/low distress.
Given our mission, we have built in structures and procedures for
continually assessing the degree to which students, teachers, and*

school leadership are flourishing and for facilitating growth when weakness is manifest.

One of the challenges we face is a potential rift between our understanding of child flourishing and a particular parent's understanding. For example, there are parents who associate child flourishing with the absence of any emotional distress. In such cases, it is assumed that if the child is distressed, the adults at the school must be doing something wrong. In contrast, we speak of the importance of delight and struggle. School days must be filled with many delightful experiences. Yet there are moments when a child is called to continued effort when head and hand are tired, when a child experiences disappointment and frustration, or when a child experiences unkindness at the hands of another child, needing to give and receive forgiveness. At Ambleside, we understand an essential aspect of child flourishing as being the ability to handle emotional distress well, stay one's best self, and return to joy quickly. We generally are not a good fit for parents whose metric for child flourishing is different than ours.

Board and community: Board members represent another of those very difficult interfaces between leadership and management requirements. Boards, like administration, interface with the legal world. Boards generally run almost entirely on slow-track activity and then, if that is not slow enough, on Robert's Rules. Boards are not all management; they represent the vision and mission of an organization. Helping board members explain a fast-track school to a slow-track world is the leadership task with the fewest resources and time available. Yet Bill gives us a RARE perspective.

We have learned that the leadership of any community has an essential priestly function to play. Pain arises in every community, and that pain invariably reaches to the feet of the leader. The priestly function of the leader is to take the pain of the community into self, offer it to Christ while staying graciously, relationally connected with hurting in the community, and thereby begin to dissipate the pain from the community. If the leader is unwilling to take the pain upon self, but rather "spits" it back into the community, invariably the community becomes increasingly unsafe and increasingly toxic.

Cultural: Maryellen and Bill will tell you that children are arriving in their schools with steadily declining social skills. The children's EQ on arrival is lower each year. More and more class time and teacher attention is needed to repair the sagging condition of the children's fast tracks. Most parents do not even faintly understand how to make relational repairs to the fast track. Parents are busy with work, broken relationships, smartphones, and other powerful distractions that limit practicing the skills they do possess.

Bill tells us:

We have always understood inspirational ideas as an essential and potent aspect of motivation. Further we have recognized the difference between an "inspirational idea" and "mere information." Information is a mere statement of fact. An idea is a new way of seeing. Ideas shape, form and transform relations. Ideas are not mere analytic abstractions from data. They are formative insights, revelations communicated mind to mind.

We are learning to put a primacy on relational dynamics. Among our staff, school principals, teachers, and students, we seek to engage with one another in ways that build trust and relational connectedness. This relational capacity building is foundational to taking and running together with the ideas that inspire us.

Personal: RARE leaders go home at night as every problem and need seeks to follow them home. Building a cozy nest where family is welcome and rest is deep requires the deepest application of fast-track training. Home requires the highest grade of fast-track skills and the most training to develop a rewarding family style. Joy remains our deepest need and most powerful motivation in our homes.

WHAT MATTERS MOST

Let us consider what businessperson and professional coach Kim Specker tells us about keeping our eye on the fast track when we lead.

> *It appears to me there could be a change when leadership no longer limits itself just to outcome-based-leadership but considers what the talent of the organization or company needs in their own personal development and maturity. The organization should look at their social responsibility to its members.*
>
> *Leadership is a tremendous responsibility. The influence and power of a leader can ignite or douse the fire in one's heart. Emotional and relational maturity is required to fan the flame of a team member's passions and strengths. What are you doing to increase your emotional and relational maturity to be the most empowering leader?*

RARE leaders understand that results matter, but they don't fix their sights on results. Fast-track leaders don't push their organizations or their ministries toward a results target. RARE leaders aim at their group's identity. Just as Jim Collins says in *Good to Great*,[2] by building a team with a great group identity, RARE leaders give their teams the best chance of getting results. In the end, the real goal is the creation of a transformative community built on belonging and identity. When we succeed in this endeavor to create a transformed identity, we cannot lose what matters most.

Brain Science for RARE Leadership

Mutual mind *states develop strong group identity*
The fast-track elevator stops at the third floor for a process that only happens here. Without this critical process we immediately stop acting like someone others would want to be around. It works so rapidly that there is no existing word for the process (although we all feel when it is missing) so it has been labeled *mutual mind*. Everything that is important for identity, group identity, motivation, discipline, activation of potential, and tracking our vision develops in a *mutual mind* state. When two brains establish a *mutual mind* state we sense the other person "gets it," "understands," "is genuine," and even "knows me."

Mutual mind states work by using mirror neurons. These neurons are activated when they "see" something that resembles their activity in another mind. To some degree mirror neurons even work across species. Your dog may notice you are sad or you may know the dog wants to go for a walk. When we are developing a group identity we are working to activate mirror neurons that think like we do in other minds and strengthen that response with relational joy.

Mutual mind states are generally developed face-to-face from gestures, facial expressions, voice tones, synchronized energy levels, and mirrored feelings. Did you ever fall hard and feel angry when others laughed at you while you were concerned you might be injured? Their laughing demonstrates a lack of *mutual mind* because although both of you know something big and unexpected just happened you do not feel a mutual concern about your body when they laugh.

Mutual mind states run faster than conscious thought. Without *mutual mind* states people do not share the same reactions, motivation, and direction. It is obvious that leaders must be really good with *mutual mind* states if they are to coordinate, lead, and motivate groups to work together at the same time, in the same direction, and with the same goals.

Traumas (and they can be surprisingly small) come from events that persistently disrupt participation in successful *mutual mind* states. Staying in *mutual mind* states is a learned and acquired skill—one that is increasingly difficult the stronger our emotions become. If we are not conditioned to stay in a *mutual mind* state when life becomes stressful or exciting, we will lose the use of our relational circuits and our fast-track elevator will jam, turning out the lights for our executive director in the penthouse. Obviously the ability to quiet rapidly, in real time, and with people present, is a big start. Restoring *mutual mind* states (often with a coach who knows how to build *mutual mind* skills and strength) builds the third-floor capacity.

Every brain has more identity potential than has been awakened. Through *mutual mind* we use that mirror potential to grow a joyful and highly motivated identity in our group. Awakening new parts of self helps grow a group identity because we realize that in this group we are more than we were before. The same *mutual mind* states and skills that build a group identity will strengthen and build fast-track functions.

DISCUSSION QUESTIONS

1. Which story in this chapter had the most connection for you? What did it teach you?

2. What do you see as the strengths and weaknesses of aiming at results as your primary target?

3. How does aiming at group identity make for a better leadership environment?

4. Have you ever worked in a results-driven ministry or organization? How did it contrast with the identity-based organizations described in this chapter? If you have worked in an identity-based culture and a results-driven culture, how would you describe the difference?

5. From the stories and explanations in this chapter, what do you see as the primary components needed in order to build a strong group identity?

Building
RARE
Leadership

CHAPTER 6

Where You Start: Imitation, Identity, Intimacy

Learning a transformation regimen

CHRIS COURSEY IS a leader lots of pastors can relate to. He never led a huge congregation, but he loved the Lord and worked really hard at being a good pastor. People generally like Chris. He smiles easily, likes to laugh, and cares about people.

But Chris admits that after several years as a counselor and pastor, a lot of the joy had gone out of his work. Like many pastors, he tried really hard to do all the right things, but he had very little peace. Something was missing, and Chris sensed it was time for a change.

Today, Chris is a joy-fueled leader who has helped to develop an in-depth training system for learning fast-track skills. However, this wasn't a transformation that happened overnight. Learning new habits takes months of training. As we learned earlier, it takes time for white brain matter to form so that good ideas actually become habits.

Several elements went into Chris's transformation from a burned-out, fear-driven leader to someone who knows how to replenish his motivation and energy through joy. Let's take a quick look at some of the key practices that went into his transformation regimen.

Imitation exercises—Chris began working with Jim Wilder to develop exercises that could help people learn many of the fast-track skills being taught in this book. Their work led to the creation of THRIVE™—a series of weeklong training events where people can learn and practice skills that help build important fast-track brain habits. To test the exercises they were developing, Chris practiced them as much as he could—with groups, with his wife, with other pastors, and with several friends. As a result he began building his emotional capacity and new habits began to take shape in his brain.

Intimacy with God—Seeking God and sharing his journey with others was critical to Chris's growth. He explains it with this:

> [Conversational prayer] was woven through all my transformation. We [Chris, his group, and his mentors] were regularly finding ways to connect with Jesus, and I sensed that He was consistently affirming who I was as a person and not just as a minister. He also began showing me my weaknesses. Instead of operating out of fear with Him, as I had done, Jesus became a safe resource.
>
> The turning point with Jesus came when my health began to deteriorate. I was on my back in bed about a week a month. During these times Jesus showed me my mixed-up loyalties. I was so loyal I assumed that if I ever left this ministry they would be carrying me out on a stretcher. He showed me that I had a lot of fear that was at the source of my problems, including fear of abandonment that distorted my loyalties.

Identity groups—Chris built relationships with people outside of his immediate community with whom he could process his issues. These "allies" helped him discover "who it was like him to be" in stressful situations—how he could bring the best of himself to these challenges. They called out what was best in him and helped him grow in his connection with Jesus. This often happened on phone calls, over coffee, or in online forums. This network was spread across the country, so there was always additional joy when they could be together in person.

One of the ways Chris's identity group helped him was to encourage him to lighten his stress load, so he could invest more time into his family and his own growth. With their encouragement, he began to say no to many of the requests for his time. People weren't used to Chris saying no. As a people pleaser, he generally said yes to everything. As the stress in his situation escalated, Chris and his wife, Jen, took a bold step and left his position. Here is what he had to say about that time in his life.

> *When I actually left the ministry, we moved in with my grand-parents. I had no job. No source of income. I felt like I had just given up everything. I had just taken this blind step with no idea of where it would lead. In a few months, things began to come together in a way I could not have imagined—a house, a job, and a new ministry.*
>
> *There was a cost to leaving. There was a cost to making changes. But everything has come together in a way I never could have imagined. Now, instead of pastoring a specific congregation and living out of fear, I am living out of joy and have a chance to raise my family and travel the world training and helping pastors. I en-joy opportunities to shepherd people including teaching elementary-aged children at church—now that can be a tough crowd!*

Today, Chris lives with a level of peace and joy he didn't know was possible when he first started this process. This isn't because his life is so much easier. A few years ago, Chris had an accident with a ladder and injured his back. As a result, he lives with chronic lower back pain as he does his best to be a husband, father to two very active boys, and stay engaged in ministry. He and Jen continue to practice a regimen of fast-track exercises and intimate times of prayer that are helping them keep their joy high in the midst of life's challenges.

In this chapter we will introduce three disciplines that help build the uncommon habits that produce RARE leaders: Imitation, Iden-tity Groups, and Intimacy with God.

IMITATION EXERCISES

Maybe you've been in a setting where you admired one of the leaders or a colleague and sought to imitate them or at least pick up clues to successfully thriving in that place. So it is with developing your fast-track skills! Fast-track skills have to be imitated. The right side of our brain doesn't learn with words. It learns by imitation and practice. The identity center of the brain has a heavy concentration of mirror neurons (which we were introduced to in the brain science section of the last chapter). Mirror neurons reflect what they see. As a result, they only learn through imitation. This is why Chris worked with me (Jim) to develop a THRIVE training program that takes place in a forum where skills can be seen and imitated.

MARY: "I LOVE THEM AND THEY LOVE WORKING HERE"

Several years ago Mary Whelchel started a radio spot called "The Christian Working Woman." Although she served as director of women's ministries at The Moody Church in Chicago, Mary never really thought of herself as a leader. She was simply passionate about getting things done for God's kingdom. "For years," she said, "I just barreled through leadership issues and learned afterward what was right and wrong. I was very project-oriented and my attitude was 'leave me alone and let me do my job!'"

> When Paul wanted to teach people how to live a mature Christian life, he knew that the best thing he could do was to offer them a role model.

As her sphere of influence grew and she needed to build a team, Mary quickly learned that she needed help if she was going to do more than simply fill holes with people who could get tasks done. Turning to a member of her board with HR experience, Mary was able to hire an emotionally mature, relationally gifted manager who helped her build a great team.

I learned so much just by watching her. This new manager was very relational. She really cared about each of the people who reported to her and demonstrated genuine interest in their families. She initiated fun activities and gave special recognition to people. She created an atmosphere where people loved coming to work.

When this highly relational manager transitioned out of her position after nine years, she helped Mary find a replacement who was just as emotionally mature and relational as she was. Today, Mary will tell you that she has "the best team in the world . . . I love them and they love working here."

When Mary first started down this path, she didn't know she even needed relational skills. After more than a decade of watching people with really great relational skills, her own have developed tremendously. This is how we learn fast-track skills. We don't just read about them in a book. We admit our own weaknesses and pay attention to people who have skills we lack. When we do this, our brains learn to imitate what we see. Mary Whelchel provides a classic example of what RARE leaders do. They use fast-track relational skills to build groups that love working together and love to tell others about their mission and their leader.

Mary's story demonstrates the power and importance of imitation. It is instructive that when Paul wanted to teach people how to live a mature Christian life, he recognized that the best thing he could do was offer them a role model. He wrote to the Philippians, "Whatever you have learned or received or heard from me, or seen in me—put it into practice" (4:9). When the Corinthians needed help dealing with some of their maturity issues, Paul sent them Timothy to remind them of Paul's example.

If you are committed to building the fast-track habits you need in order to become a rare leader, it is important to identify which skills you are lacking—which requires a measure of humility—and find people in your circle who have those skills. They may not be more skilled than you in much else, but they are good at the skill you need. Watching these people and interacting with them is a crucial part of any growth regimen focused on building RARE habits. (You can also make the investment to go through the THRIVE skill training in order to jump-start this process. See page 221.)

INTIMACY WITH GOD

If you had the chance to interview most of the people whose stories are shared in this book, you would discover that at some point most of them would speak of the impact their times with God had on them. They might say something like, "I live with so much more joy now! I am less controlled by negative emotions and quicker to handle problems relationally."

DEVELOPING INTIMACY WITH GOD

John Maxwell is among the most widely read leadership experts in the world. What many people don't know is that one of the first books he ever wrote was about prayer.[1] As a college student Maxwell developed the habit of spending the hour after lunch alone with God—just a Bible, a pen, and a spiral notebook. He spent time praying and listening. As a pastor, one of his first priorities was the development of a prayer team that saturated his ministry in prayer.

Bill Hybels, the founding pastor of Willow Creek Community Church, has developed a similar approach to building intimacy with God. He describes his decision to develop a disciplined approach to prayer in his book *Too Busy Not to Pray*:

> *Prayer has not always been my strong suit. For many years, even as senior pastor of a large church, I knew more about prayer than I ever practiced in my own life. I have a racehorse temperament, and the tugs of self-sufficiency and self-reliance are very real to me. I didn't want to get off the fast track long enough to find out what prayer is all about.*
>
> *But the Holy Spirit gave me a leading so direct that I couldn't ignore it, argue against it or disobey it. The leading was to explore, study and practice prayer until I finally understood it. I obeyed that leading. I read fifteen or twenty major books on prayer, some old and some new. I studied almost every passage on prayer in the Bible.*
>
> *And then I did something really radical: I prayed.*

It has been twenty years since I began taking time to pray, and my prayer life has been transformed. The greatest fulfillment has not been the list of miraculous answers to prayers I have received, although that has been wonderful. The greatest thrill has been the qualitative difference in my relationship with God.[2]

Developing a relationship with God requires learning the art of conversational prayer. The idea that God can and does want to speak to His children is one of the foundations of spiritual maturity. In his classic book *The Pursuit of God*, A. W. Tozer encouraged us to pray for intimacy with God and suggests the following prayer.

Lord, teach me to listen. The times are noisy and my ears are weary with the thousand raucous sounds which continuously assault them. Give me the spirit of the boy Samuel when he said to Thee, "Speak, for thy servant heareth." Let me hear Thee speaking in my heart. Let me get used to the sound of Thy Voice, that its tones may be familiar when the sounds of earth die away and the only sound will be the music of Thy speaking Voice. Amen.

If there were a thousand distractions in Tozer's day (he ministered primarily from the 1920s into the '50s), one can only imagine how many distractions the modern leader faces that call him away from the pursuit of God's presence. Spiritually mature people of all ages have built a habit of intimacy with God that Tozer calls "spiritual receptivity." It is the practice of paying attention to what God is whispering to our hearts.

We intuitively understand that mature believers should be better practiced in the art of intimacy with God and recognizing His still small voice within than those who are just beginning their journey. As leaders it is crucial that we develop our "spiritual receptivity" by learning to practice the presence of God.

So is there anything we have learned from brain science that might be able to help us with our spiritual disciplines? Of course! God designed us for relationship with Him. It would make no sense if our brains were not crafted by the Almighty to facilitate the experience of His presence.

In general, listening is a difficult art for leaders to master. We like to be on the move and get things done. One of the reasons we struggle with listening is that it requires strong right-brain, fast-track skills. If I only listen with my slow-track left brain, I merely process information. Most of us are pretty good at this. Someone comes in and talks to us while we are watching TV or reading emails, and we listen to them without ever making eye contact or engaging with them emotionally. Our slow track can repeat the information we heard, but there was no relational engagement. The fast-track tasks of reading people's emotions and synchronizing with them are non-verbal skills and vital to the listening process.

In a similar way, listening to God is not primarily about listening for words. It is about sensing His voice with the fast-track part of our brain.[3]

Here are some practical steps that can help us grow our ability to recognize God's voice and improve our spiritual receptivity.

1. **Quiet.** Just as we need to turn off the TV or stop looking at email if we want to truly listen to others, we need to do the same if we want to improve our connection with God. Scheduling regular times for this type of conversational prayer is often called having a "quiet time" for a reason.

2. **Scripture Reading.** An often overlooked facet of spending time in the Word is that it orients our souls around the nature and ways of God. As we soak in the Word, His Spirit uses those themes to guide our minds toward His interests. The more time you spend listening to a certain composer, the more familiar you become with his style and the more you recognize his influence on other musicians.

3. **Appreciation.** The psalmist told us to enter into God's gates with thanksgiving and into His courts with praise.[4] Giving

and receiving appreciation builds healthy relationships at a human level. It just makes sense that it would be good for our relationship with God as well. From a brain science perspective, it is interesting to note that appreciation turns on our mental receptors. It is as if appreciation flips a switch that turns on the relational part of our brain and prepares us for interaction with other people. It can do the same for our interaction with God as well.

Several years ago, I (Marcus) lost my mother to kidney failure. She was eighty-five, as was my father. You can imagine my surprise when my dad remarried at the age of eighty-nine! His new bride is a wonderful woman who served Lord faithfully her entire life. When you meet her, you can't help but be impressed with her joy, her peace, and her deep love for the Lord. One of her secrets is that for decades, she has maintained a gratitude journal. She has dozens of them. Every day, she records her reasons for gratitude and sets her heart on appreciation. Just as the Psalmist practiced appreciation as his key to entrance into God's presence, so it can serve as a wonderful warmup for relational time with God.

4. **Writing.** For years, my father was the international director of Freedom in Christ Ministries, founded by Dr. Neil T. Anderson. Dr. Anderson was one of the first people I heard clearly describe his practice of writing in a notebook during his times of prayer. In fact, he often used two notebooks. In one he wrote his prayers. In the other, he wrote his distractions.

Quieting ourselves to pray is often interrupted by distracting thoughts. Sometimes these are as simple as "you need to change the oil." Other times they are accusing thoughts from the enemy like, "You're never going to learn how to do this," or, "God is never going to speak to you." Anderson learned to write both kinds of thoughts into his distraction notebook. Some were thoughts to be taken captive. Others turned into a "to-do" list. After years of struggling to spend more than five or ten minutes in relational prayer with God, he soon found it no trouble at all to enjoy an hour or more with God.

5. **Sharing**. When it comes to recognizing and discerning God's voice, it is a good practice to share what you sense God is saying with others. In fact, it is dangerous to rely solely on your own judgment. Group discernment provides an important safety net as we learn to sense God's guidance and relational presence in our lives. I (Marcus) often share my journaling with trusted friends and rely on their feedback to help me discern what God may be saying to me. They often help me recognize when God is pointing out areas where I may be stuck or new insights he wants me to learn.

The purpose of building intimacy with God is not to get His input on our decisions so that we will be more successful leaders. That does happen along the way, but it is not why we pursue intimacy. We do this for the relational connection it brings, the healing it facilitates, and the peace that comes from a deeper walk with Him.[5]

IDENTITY GROUPS: A TEAM OF ALLIES

I (Marcus) have found that if I want to establish a new habit or develop a new skill, the first thing I need to do is join a group that is working on that skill. If it is art, I need to join an art class. If it is gardening, I need to join a gardening club. If it is tennis, I need to join a league. I find that if I don't do this, I don't follow through. Being part of a group brings an intrinsic motivation with it. There are simply things I will do because I belong to a group that I won't do if there is no one joining me.

When I was first starting out in ministry, I used to set aside two hours every Thursday to meet with a retired gentleman from the church. All we did was Bible memory for those two hours. I was memorizing the book of John, and he volunteered to help me. Each week, he would read a line from the text and I would repeat it three times, then he would feed me the next line and I would repeat that three times, then I would put the lines together and repeat them. He would correct and encourage me and seemed to find as much joy in watching me master the material as I did in learning it. We found that within two hours of doing this, I could generally plow my way through a whole chapter. Knowing that he would be in that quiet, comfortable room in the church each Thursday gave me the motivation I needed to keep showing up. I am also a verbal processor and the relational connection made a big difference. By the end of the year, I could quote the entire book of John backward and forward. That would never have happened without his help.

For any real transformation to take place, you are going to need a team that is committed to a common goal. We have been calling this team your "identity group." If you choose to call it something else, that is fine. Make it your own. However, there are certain qualities that this team needs to have in order for it to work.

• **This is a group of allies, not an accountability group.** Its purpose is not to get you to sign a pledge committing yourself to make certain changes and then hold your feet to the fire to make sure you follow through. Such fear-based systems grow out of a results-oriented model and represent the antithesis of what we're trying to teach. The first person I (Marcus) heard discuss this principle was John Eldredge. He called his team "allies" and "brothers." They liked to say they were "barbarians not bureaucrats." I like that. It was a phrase that reminded them of their core values. They weren't building an organization, they were on a journey. They wanted to keep their identity and core values clear. They were in this together to help each other on a common journey of transformation and discovery.

> We don't need people to beat us up when we fail. Most of us are pretty good at doing that ourselves.

Allies are the sort of people you want with you in the foxhole when you are in a battle. They aren't there to evaluate you. They are there to call out what is best in you. Sometimes they do it just by what they model. When you see "Joe" get up out of the foxhole and engage the enemy, it gives you the courage to do the same. When you see "Barbara" open up about a weakness and observe the tender response she receives, it emboldens you to step up and be vulnerable as well. Sometimes they do it with their words. They validate your emotions. They offer new perspectives. They let you know they are in this with you. Whether by words or deeds, these are people who help you act like yourself when life gets hard.

• **This group must be tender toward weakness.** We generally don't need people to beat us up when we fail. Most of us are pretty good at doing that to ourselves. Most accountability groups fall apart when people start to fail at keeping their promises. They know they have failed and don't see the point in showing up somewhere just to be reminded of their failure and told to do better when they don't know *how* to do better. Groups that are tender toward weakness (V) validate emotions, (C) comfort us with new perspectives and possible solutions, and help us (R) repattern so that we can act like ourselves (VCR).[6] Groups that are tender toward weakness are good at the VCR process.

• **This group needs to be committed to seeking God.** True transformation happens when God and His people are interacting together. I (Marcus) often share from my journaling with members of my group—sometimes together, but usually one at a time. I rely on them to help me sort through what I sense God may be saying. On occasion, especially if it involves a memory from my past or a powder-keg issue, I also look to them to help me connect with God and work through things until I feel God's *shalom*—that settled sense that God has given me enough of His perspective to be at peace.

• **This group can be spread out across the world.** With today's Internet meeting options and smartphones, identity groups don't have to be local. In this group I am looking for peers and people who have skills I lack. I (Jim) have met in person with a team of prayer partners for several years. I have also had a group of allies spread out across the country who stay connected with one another. These are the people I go to for support and encouragement. I (Marcus) have a collection of allies scattered around the country that I call on a regular basis. We get together in person when we can. These are people I can tell anything to because I know I am going to get a tender response to my weakness. They may end up challenging me to do hard things, but they will do it because they are calling out my true heart and how they know it is like me to act.

The interesting thing about relational skills is that they have to be built . . . in relationship! You can't just read a book and try to change in isolation. It doesn't work. Start putting your team together, even if it is just one other person in the beginning. Ask God to bring it together. He already has a plan for helping with this.

TRANSFORMATION TAKES TIME

In this part of the book, we are exploring the four uncommon habits that characterize RARE leaders. Throughout these chapters, we will make reference to the importance of imitation exercises, the pursuit of intimacy with God, and participation in identity groups.

Building new habits isn't easy. It takes time, and we have found that without all three of these key elements you aren't going to get there. Leaders are often in a hurry for change, which is understandable, but some things can't be rushed and shortcuts cause problems. I (Jim) learned this the hard way as a youngster. I once found a monarch butterfly in the process of emerging from its cocoon. Being the helpful sort of person I am, I decided to jump in and speed up the process for this poor, struggling insect. I got him out more quickly than he could have done on his own, but the results were disastrous. The poor bug's wings were not straight and it couldn't fly! While my intentions were good, taking shortcuts did not accomplish what needed to happen. It is the same with learning fast-track habits. You can't simply choose to be mature. But there are choices you can make that will help build the habits that can transform your life, your marriage, your parenting, and your leadership competence.

Brain Science for RARE Leadership

The four "engines" of attachment

The attachment styles that characterize level one of the fast-track system are one of the most researched topics in psychology. The same four patterns appear across all cultures and races.

When the first two years of life are joyful we develop pattern one—*secure attachment*. These "joy bonds" provide a very stable and powerful way of relating to our world both inside and outside of our bodies.

The other three patterns are all fearful patterns of seeing the world and motivating ourselves. Pattern two is a fearful style that avoids others and stays independent. Pattern three is a clingy style that always wants "in." Pattern four is disorganized and we never know what will upset them.

Because attachment patterns are the most persistent of all the measureable traits across the lifespan, people expect their group identity (their people) will be motivated like they are—1) working together joyfully, 2) taking care of themselves (fear of other is rarely admitted), 3) trying to stay "in" with everyone (fear of loss or rejection), or 4) avoiding whatever might go wrong next.

The advantage of the fear-based systems is that they accelerate quickly (but I have to get mad and yell to get anyone to move), while the disadvantage is that under any tension at all they lose mutual mind and forget entirely about acting like themselves.

The advantage of a joy-based group identity is that it "runs cool" most of the time and has amazing resilience, focus, direction, and self-restoring capacity. These patterns are the same for all groups, cultures, languages, and ages (over eighteen months of age). Styles of expression vary greatly but the "engines" are the same.

Leaders must find and strengthen the engine their group will use. This is one of the central tasks of leadership. The three fear engines, like the joy engine, all run faster than conscious thought and are shaped and controlled through mutual-mind state skills. The brain will default to fear without being trained properly but the brain is also wired to prefer the joy engine when training is available. This means that across the life span engines can upgrade to joy, and when they do they become more stable, run cooler, and always appreciate those who helped them upgrade to a better personal and group identity.

Training individuals and groups how to validate, comfort, and recover or repattern (VCR) turns off fearful alarms, reduces reactivity, and prevents people from keeping out of sight when there are issues to resolve.

The studies of securely attached infants (about two years old) who face pain and problems with calm and cool-running brains reveal that these children spontaneously validate and comfort *themselves* aloud. Speaking aloud allows them to have the same effect on themselves that hearing their parents validate and comfort them would have, and this sets the pattern for life. Insecure children do not validate and comfort themselves. We have added repatterning to validation and comfort to help convert people to more secure and stable modes. It is important that the new pattern becomes one of saying validating and comforting things to myself when I need to quiet and cool my brain.

DISCUSSION QUESTIONS/EXERCISES

1. Were there any elements of Chris Coursey's story to which you could relate? When have you felt like you were functioning beyond your emotional capacity?

2. Who do you know in your circles who have relational skills it would be good to imitate? What do they do well that you would like to learn?

3. Have you ever practiced any form of interactive prayer? Try journaling this week and sharing what you write with one or two people you trust. This is a good way to start building an identity group.

4. Do you already have a group where you feel free to take off your mask and be real? How many people can you name who would be supportive and helpful in the process of admitting your weaknesses and joining you on a regimen of maturity development?

Remain Relational

Keeping relationships bigger than problems

EVERYONE KNOWS THAT being relational is essential to leadership. Ever since Dale Carnegie wrote his classic work *How to Win Friends and Influence People,* leadership books have been filled with relationship advice. The focus of this chapter is on the tension between remaining relational and solving problems. Emotionally immature leaders have almost no capacity to remain relational in the face of big problems. They isolate, they blame, they get angry—and they usually lose themselves in an addiction. RARE leaders are the ones who find relational ways to solve problems and thus, keep relationships bigger than problems.

MIKE: KEEPING RELATIONSHIPS BIGGER THAN PROBLEMS

I (Marcus) have a friend—we'll call him Mike—who runs a small, but effective, advisory team. He is an emotionally mature leader who has done a great job of building a strong group identity for his team. In a field like his, it would be easy to define success simply in terms of results and let problems get bigger than relationships. Recently Mike changed his entire approach to evaluating team members. It used to be that they simply set target numbers for how many products and services each administrative person needed to generate for the business. This was a very results-oriented approach that led to a lot of frustration, resentment, and anxiety, because you can't always control whether people want to buy your product or enroll in a service.

Most of these emotions got bottled up and hidden from the boss but would be freely expressed to other coworkers.

This didn't make for the greatest work environment. The new system was based on a clearly communicated group identity that said, "We simplify and improve the lives of our clients while striving to reach our own potential." Instead of basing evaluations on outcomes or numbers, evaluations were built on process. Targets were set for how many client contacts were made and how carefully the company strategy for doing business was followed. Unlike the number of services enrolled or products sold, these were all activities that could be controlled by the employees, so the system felt fair to everyone. It alleviated a lot of stress at the office, and revenue numbers have actually increased.

Before coming to work for Mike, one lady in his office had worked for an organization whose boss was known for being very tough to work with. Shortly after joining his team she made a costly mistake. It cost the company and the team a lot of money. At her old job, she would have been shamed publicly and potentially fired. So you can imagine her anxiety when Mike called her into his office. She could hardly look at him and just kept waiting for the inevitable eruption. Instead he told her, "Look, you made a mistake. It was a big mistake, but it was an accident. Try not to let this happen again. I just want you to know you are still part of this team and we value what you have to offer."

She was overjoyed and became emotional. After being in a job where she had to walk on eggshells around the boss, she was prepared for the worst and couldn't believe the tenderness with which her weakness was handled. In this problem situation, Mike remained relational, acted like himself, and helped everyone return to joy. That's what emotionally mature bosses do. So, what do you think happened to this woman's level of motivation after this? Do you think she came to work with joy or with fear? This is the power of emotionally mature leadership. It makes doing even hard jobs enjoyable.

JOSEPH: MOTIVATED BY ANGER

Prior to learning the habits of a RARE lifestyle, Joseph was an auto business owner living in fear and anger and not even realizing it. There was a decent dose of guilt and shame thrown in as well. Like a lot of businessmen, his main priority was the financial security of his family. Yet it was problems in his family that first led him to look for answers. He attended a Deeper Walk training event where I (Marcus) was teaching and got introduced to the Life Model. Soon, he and his wife attended the "level one" training event that Jim and his team had created. The skills he learned there changed his life. They not only made a profound impact on his personal and family life, they affected the way he did business and the way he approached life altogether.

Like a lot of us, Joseph often motivated himself with anger and considered it normal. It wasn't unusual for him to use self-talk like: "Come on, you can do better than that! What's the matter with you? Get your butt in gear or you're going to blow this! Do it or else!" Since he only knew how to motivate himself with fear and anger, guess what he used to motivate the team in his business?

You have to understand, Joseph was a nice guy. Nobody thought of him as an ogre and people generally liked him. But there was something broken inside, and when Joseph was pushed or situations overwhelmed him, he stopped acting like himself and let problems get bigger than relationships.

Before his Life Model training, Joseph often avoided the normal conflicts inside himself and the pressure that inevitably comes up while managing a business and people. His mindset was, "I'll do my job. You do yours." When frustration became unavoidable, anger was his default communication style. Deeper Walk helped Joseph deal with his wounds and THRIVE training helped him develop the RARE skills that transformed his relationships.

Recently, a problem arose at his business that Joseph was able to handle in a way that kept the

He said to his employee, "I know this is not the kind of person you want to be."

relationship bigger than the problem. A senior technician who had been with the company a long time and was close to retirement began to take advantage of the fact that Joseph was not on-site as his sons took over more of the business. This experienced technician was being disrespectful (especially to the younger son with oversight responsibility) and was not following through on important deadlines. Here's what Joseph did—and what he didn't do.

He knew action had to be taken but felt equipped to bring life to the situation.

He *didn't avoid the problem* and he didn't use anger or fear of threats to resolve it.

He *protected the employee's honor.*

He *focused on the relationship.* "You and I have known each other a long time. You have added a lot of value to this company and to me personally."

He *kept the employee's true heart perspective in sight* while addressing difficult issues.

He *spoke to the man's heart.* "I know this is not the person you want to be. I know the kind of person you really are. You're a hard worker, respectful, and love to help people. I'm just asking you to act like yourself." Joseph was reminding his employee to act like himself and enjoy the freedom that comes from living out of a true heart.

It worked. The man responded really well and there was a noticeable rise in the level of respect for team members after that. Joseph's relationship with this man was stronger than ever after this. Joseph had learned how to remain relational in a difficult situation and keep the relationship bigger than the problem.

HOW DO YOU MAP OUT YOUR WORLD?

Leaders who are dominated by fear will map out the world around them in terms of problems to be solved. Their brains by default lock on to whatever is scary or potentially bad in their environment, and that is what gets all of their attention.

On the other hand, joy-oriented people map out their world in terms of what is good in life. They excel at appreciation and (as Paul encouraged us) fix their minds on what is lovely, excellent, and praiseworthy. These leaders don't ignore problems. In fact, like Joseph, they are more likely to stop avoiding problems than fear-based leaders. However, they deal with problems in a relational way. Their goal is to solve problems in a way that makes relationships stronger when they are finished.

This does not come naturally for leaders who lack maturity. Quite the opposite. In fact, emotionally immature people are often quite good at turning their relationships into problems that need to be solved. This is what happens when relationships become codependent. People bond out of fear of losing a relationship. Saving the relationship is the problem to be solved. The very process of turning the relationship into a problem works against any hope of saving it.

As I (Marcus) write this, I have several problems I am facing that would make it easy to stop being relational:

- Shortage of money for staff
- Marriage retreat preparation for this weekend
- Board retreat in two weeks (lots of details still in the air)
- Deadlines for writing
- Needing to find a new venue for a fall event (the original location had to be changed)
- Following up on an invitation to help plan and lead a conference six months from now in another state
- Technical problems with our video production
- Important issues that have been put on the back burner in order to deal with urgent issues
- Handling emails from people with difficult counseling situations

The list could go on. In the middle of all of this my family has had to deal with a medical crisis that made us drop everything in order to bring my father-in-law into our home for the week. Now we are starting to research treatment options and long-term care possibilities. Many of you can relate. Leaders often have more on their plates at any given time than they can realistically handle. Many of the issues are emotionally taxing and relationally challenging. Trying to balance all of that with family needs and unexpected crises can just be par for the course. It can also make things break down internally and relationally.

Partly because I am working on a chapter called "remain relational," I have been intentionally doing my best to keep my relationships bigger than my problems this week. That means connecting with my wife at an emotional level and not just a problem-solving level. It means taking advantage of opportunities to laugh with my teenage son when he walks into the room with a funny video he just found. It means canceling some appointments and saying no to some otherwise important tasks in order to be relationally present with my wife's dad. It also means making plans to share my own emotions with some peers later this week. (I'm anticipating that I will need to vent!) I also took time to read my Bible and write in my journal this morning to give myself a chance to hear from God. I felt like He was telling me this was a chance to practice some skills I have been working on and to trust that He wasn't letting all of this happen in order to punish me or let me feel the consequences of my prior folly (my mind tends to go that direction). His goodness and love are still pursuing me and especially on days like this when I need it the most.

SIGNS YOU HAVE SHUT DOWN RELATIONALLY

In chapter 3 we introduced the image of an elevator in the right brain that moved information through the fast track. Another way to think about this process is to imagine that we have an "on/off" switch on the back of our necks. When the switch is in the "on" position, we are able to engage relationally and get in sync with the emotions of the people around us. However, when the switch is off, our capacity to remain relational disappears. The fast-track elevator is stuck. This switch controls the relational circuits (RCs) in our brain.

Dr. Karl Lehman, a psychiatrist and friend of ours, has identified several tests for determining if your relational brain circuits are off.[1] Here are some of the signs you have shut down relationally.

1. You don't feel like being around someone you normally like.
2. You just want to make a person or problem go away.
3. Your mind is locked on to something upsetting.
4. You become aggressive in the way you interrogate, judge, or fix people.
5. You don't want to make eye contact.
6. You feel like it is their fault if they get hurt by something you do or say.

It is possible to operate out of the slow track of the brain with our relational brain circuits off, but our fast-track system will not be leading us. When our RCs are off, our fast track is off-line. In order to remain relational, act like ourselves, and return to joy we need to have our RCs on.

In the next section of this chapter, we will look at four simple strategies you can use to get your relational brain circuits engaged so that you can remain relational and keep your relationships bigger than your problems.

RELATIONAL STRATEGIES

These four simple strategies can help you get started in growing the skills that build habit #1—remaining relational. You can use the word CAKE to remember them.

Curiosity

"I'm curious." Simple words, but powerful. One of the best ways to remain relational is to use these words to start a sentence. Curiosity is a clear sign that you are in relational mode. When your relational circuits are on, your curiosity about life and people kicks in. When your circuits are off, you stop thinking relationally and only see problems. Being curious about something can help you remain relational. When a board member shows up at a meeting fuming about a problem, and convinced it is your fault, how do you react? Are you defensive and problem-focused? Or do you keep the relationship bigger than the problem, remaining curious? You might say, "I'm curious if you handle problems like this at work?" or "I can see you're upset. I'm curious if you notice the effect your tone is having on the group?" or perhaps, "I'm curious if this situation reminds you of another problem in the past that didn't end well?"

In a talk on handling criticism at a Deeper Walk conference, Neil T. Anderson told of a time he was confronted by a member of the church he pastored. This woman had taken the time to write out all of her grievances with him, and it took more than a single sheet of paper to write them all down! His natural instinct was to be defensive. Instead he said, "You know, I bet it took a lot of courage to come in here and say all of that. I wonder [i.e., curious] if there is something underneath all of this you might want to talk about." Using curiosity instead of defensiveness kept the relationship bigger than the problem and demonstrated emotional maturity.

When God showed up in the Garden after Adam and Eve's sin, He expressed curiosity: "Where are you? . . . Who told you that you were naked?" (Genesis 3:9, 11). Asking questions may have been one way the LORD was seeking to maintain a relationship even as His creatures had been discovered in their sin. This is in keeping with God's character since even in His holiness He seeks to restore and enjoy relational connection with His people.

> Appreciation attracts, while resentment repels.

You can test whether your relational switch is in the on or the off position by checking your curiosity level. You can also turn your switch on by asking curiosity questions, like "How do you feel about this?" or "I'm curious if you have given thought to the next steps here."

It should be pointed out that curiosity and sarcasm are opposites. Curiosity wants to know what is going on inside someone and what it would take to help them connect relationally. Sarcasm may use curiosity, but it does so to try to disconnect relationally. Sarcasm says things like, "I'm curious. Are you always that stupid?" This is not keeping relationships bigger than problems!

Appreciation

Two powerful forces in any relationship are appreciation and resentment. Appreciation attracts, while resentment repels. They are like two magnets. When facing the right direction, they attract one another. If you flip them around, they repel each other. It is the same way in our relationships. Sincere appreciation wakes up the relational circuits in us and in the person receiving the appreciation. It turns our switch to the on position and, if the other person receives the appreciation, it turns on their circuits as well. On the other hand, one of the fastest ways to shut down somebody's relational circuits is with resentment and contempt.

A recent study divided marriages into two categories: "masters" and "disasters." To qualify as a "master" marriage it had to still be healthy after six years. To fall into the category of disaster, the marriage had to have already ended or be relationally unhealthy after six years. The role of appreciation in creating "master" marriages was significant. It was described as a "certain habit of the mind" that was intentionally cultivated. These couples are scanning their social environment for things they can appreciate and say thank you for. They are building this culture of respect and appreciation very purposefully.

In sharp contrast to this practice of appreciation, disaster marriages practiced contempt. In fact, they found that contempt was "the number one factor that tears couples apart. People who are focused on criticizing their partners miss a whopping 50 percent of positive things their partners are doing and can even create negativity when it's not there!"[2]

Not only is appreciation a powerful force in marriage, it is one of the most powerful forces in any relational setting. Emotionally mature leaders will always be grateful people. They excel at finding what is praiseworthy in every situation.

Emotionally immature leaders find it much easier to spot reasons for criticism than praise. They don't just forget to say "Thank you." They are ungrateful. Paul wrote that in the last days emotional immaturity would dominate our world. He wrote, "People will be lovers of self, lovers of money, proud, arrogant, abusive, disobedient to their parents, ungrateful, unholy."[3]

As Paul McCabe writes in *Feed the Good Dog*, "Ungrateful people breed negativity. No one gets any pleasure from giving to an ungrateful person. When you show appreciation, the object of your attention blossoms and flourishes."[4]

As Steve Brunkhorst says, "Feeling appreciated is one of the most important needs that people have. When you share with someone your appreciation and gratitude, they will not forget you. Appreciation will return to you many times."[5]

Appreciation also helps to build a good group identity. When people feel appreciated, they feel like they belong to and are valued by the group.

Kindness

Kindness can be defined as "shared joy." It is doing things that create joy for someone else. In the process your joy grows as well. According to this same study,

> One of the telltale signs of the disaster couples studied was their inability to connect over each other's good news. When one person in the relationship shared the good news of, say, a promotion at work with excitement, the other would respond with wooden disinterest by checking his watch or shutting the conversation down with a comment like, "That's nice."[6]

Shared joy is perhaps the most powerful relational experience that exists. Joy is always relational and the more that it is shared, the more it multiplies and amplifies other good emotions. When we lack sufficient relational joy, we will always turn to other cravings to try to fill the void. That is usually when we end up in trouble.

Envelope Conversations

An envelope conversation sticks the problem that needs to be discussed into the envelope of relationship. There is a simple pattern to it. You start with the history and importance of the relationship, then you discuss the problem, finally you end with the hope that the relationship will be even stronger once the problem is solved. You can also think of this as a sandwich conversation. You put the meat of the "problem" between the two slices of "relational" bread.

This is not the same as saying something positive before you say something negative (though that is not a bad habit). This is about making the relationship bigger than the problem. The goal in such a conversation is not simply the solving of the problem but the restoring of the relationship. When a relationship is healthy, it deals with problems, and it solves them in the most productive and least harmful way. When we are relational, we tend to think about what is best for everyone and not just what is best for ourselves because we see others in our group as a part of ourselves.

I (Marcus) recently talked with a woman who used to struggle to stay relational during conflict. When she got triggered and felt afraid, she would use shame and fear to control people. There was often a bite in her words and she would say things like, "Really, you're a Christian and you let that happen? What were you thinking, anyway?" Even though she was a psychologist, she needed to grow in her skills at managing her emotions when she was triggered. She was just more sophisticated with the words she used to control people.

However, after working through the Life Model, attending all three tracks of THRIVE and learning the RARE skills THRIVE training teaches, she has found herself caring more deeply about people and handling conflict in a way that keeps relationships bigger than problems. Recently, she found herself in a situation that in the past would have triggered an angry response and she would have most likely used shame to motivate the person to fix the situation. She was helping her daughter in the process of having a mortgage approved. Three days before closing date, someone dropped the ball in a big way and it looked like the loan would not be approved.

Her daughter was confused, angry, and overwhelmed. In the past she might have called the company to give them a piece of her mind, "What's wrong with you idiots? Why can't you get your act together? Don't you know what you're putting my daughter through?" Instead, she wrote an email to this individual's supervisor that was supportive and appreciative of the team, yet brought the problem to his attention and asked for his special intervention to make the loan happen. Their whole team then worked very hard to pull off the desired outcome.

After the closing, she found that she truly cared about the young man who had not managed the situation well. Even though these people were strangers, she wanted to find a way to process the situation with him, to affirm his efforts and help him be better at the job as a result of this experience. Normally, her response would have been an impatient, "Just give me the mortgage, I'm never working with you people again." This time her response was, "I can tell you are good people who made a mistake. I think we can navigate this problem and do business together in the future." She even went a step further and offered some coaching help to the young man who had dropped the ball. Now that's what I call keeping a relationship bigger than the problem!

WHAT *HESED* LOOKS LIKE

Hesed is one of the most common words used in the Old Testament to describe God. You could translate it "sticky love." It is the sort of love you can't shake off. It sticks to you through every high and low, every success and failure, every malfunction and sin. The New Testament word for *hesed* is *agape*. It is the kind of love Christians are commanded to demonstrate for one another, and even for our enemies. It is a sacrificial love that seeks relationship regardless of the problems involved.

As a young man, I (Jim) spent one summer working at a camp that often saw people from the inner city of Chicago come to the country to gain a different perspective on life. One inner-city group that came there was composed entirely of senior citizens. What happened that week taught me a life lesson about emotional maturity and the biblical idea of *hesed*.

One older lady came to my attention when we took the campers for meals. It was the practice at this camp to have two lines at mealtime. Those seniors who needed a walker to get around got the short line by the door. Everyone else was in the other line. Our first meal of the week the lady I noticed rushed ahead, knocking over people with walkers until she reached the front of the line, where she pushed at the door. I reprimanded her. She obviously could walk fine and should be in the other line.

But it was as though I, and my words to her, did not exist. She stared ahead demanding food and rushed through the door the second the staff opened the lunch line. The surprised staff jumped out of the way while she grabbed food and devoured it before anyone else could eat. This happened at every meal and the only way to manage the situation was for counselors to form a human shield in front of the walker brigade before she could knock them over.

To make matters worse, this woman stunk and could be smelled for quite a distance. She absolutely refused to take a shower. Within a few days the female counselors could take the stench no longer, so a group of them forcibly dragged her into one of the shower stalls. The fight and noise could be heard all around, but the campers and the staff were grateful for the result.

Another camper who drew my attention was an elderly man who was poised, dapper, and highly educated. He spoke at least seventeen languages and spoke to me thoughtfully and intelligently about many subjects. One evening I sat down with him on a hilltop at the camp as he explained the differences between Hungarian and other languages. As we spoke, the annoying woman walked by, and I mentally noticed I could not smell her this time. I took the opportunity to comment on how she had become the bane of the camp and had been wreaking havoc all week.

"That's my wife," he said quietly.

I was shocked and speechless. This was beyond

> "People say I should put her in a home, but I just can't do it. I remember her."

belief, and I was as embarrassed as I could be for my comments. The old man looked at me a moment; then, turning his arm, held out his left hand. I stared a few moments until he pointed to a long number tattooed there.

"We were both held in Nazi concentration camps," he explained. "She was once a concert pianist. She toured Europe—a lovely, talented, caring woman. But in the camp [Ravensbruck, I think he said] they cut away her brain a piece at a time without anesthesia. I was in Auschwitz. When I found her after the war she was like this."

We sat in silence and I stared at his arm. After a bit he said, "People say I should put her in a home, but I just can't do it. I remember her."

Almost thirty years had passed with no improvement. As I sat thinking, my mind flashed on the camp showers in a large room with showerheads all around. They looked like the pictures I had seen of the so-called "showers" where Jews were gassed. I thought about the lines for meals. I thought about the glazed look in her eye and her constant panic. Then there was this quiet man, sitting by me on the hill.

The old gentleman knew the talented pianist. He loved her with that enduring, "sticky" love the Bible calls *hesed*. This Hebrew word is used 253 times in the Old Testament, usually to describe God. In fact, it could be argued that no quality describes God's character more completely than *hesed*. The word refers to a love that simply does not go away, no matter how annoying or rebellious we are or how much pain we cause our Heavenly Father. It is the kind of love that makes relationships bigger than problems.

God demonstrated this kind of love toward Israel even when they were stiff-necked and rebellious to the point that God had to issue her a certificate of divorce and send her away.[7] Some Old Testament scholars have suggested that the word *hesed* means something like "covenant loyalty," but that completely misses the power of the word. The husband whose wife had been altered so dramatically during her captivity certainly demonstrated covenant loyalty for his wife. But there is a sacrificial depth to this kind of love that is only found in the most emotionally mature among us.

YOUR PRIMARY RELATIONSHIP

In the immature brain, pain turns off the relational circuits. In stark contrast, the mature brain has developed the capacity to remain relational in spite of pain. This is why RARE leaders regularly ask themselves, "How do I remain relational and act like myself in spite of the problem I am facing and the pain that I feel?"

This is not only true about our relationships with other people; it is true about our relationship with God. One of the most important applications of this skill is to be sure that I never lose track of my primary relationship with God. I don't want to lose my sense of God's presence in the midst of any problems or hardship. That is why God tells us to pray about everything and to cast all of our cares upon Him. He wants us to keep our relationship with Him bigger than the problems we face.

Developing relational skills doesn't mean that we will save every relationship. Even God hasn't managed to pull this off. But He never stops thinking relationally about the problems that must be solved. His thoughts are always driven by *hesed*. As a leader, God is building a group identity for His people so they will know how to suffer well.

Brain Science for RARE Leadership

Amplifiers in the brain

We cannot pay equal attention to everything. Out of all the activities around and within us we must ignore some and amplify others in order to achieve our most desired trait—focused attention.

Different parts of the brain amplify different mental interests, of which some are conscious (the sound of the wind outside your window as you read this) and others are not (like blood pressure). We also compare the intensity of various signals to decide what is important. For instance, if at 3 p.m. you notice your car needs an oil change and that your daughter's birthday party is starting you cannot do both. The signal that has received the most amplification will direct what you do next—go to her party or the garage. Dr. Oliver Sacks writes about people with brain damage to the fast track who are unable to decide which is more important—birthday or oil change—although fully aware of both. This inability to compare is due to localized damage in the penthouse where the "executive" has physically died.

In essence, the brain depends on steady levels of amplification to make good comparisons and decide what is more important at any given time. There are various sources of distortion and uneven amplification that leaders should understand as this distortion is the cause of a huge number of leadership failures and group-identity conflicts.

1. Attachment pain—This term refers to losses of someone we love. The effect of loss is that every other kind of pain becomes much more intensely felt. Leaders with excellent judgment often make judgment errors while feeling attachment pain. When anticipating my father's death, I told my board not to let me make large decisions for a year after my father's passing.

2. Incompletely processed memories—The right brain processes experiences from raw emotions into wisdom by sending the experience through the "mutual mind" process. When mutual mind is not achieved, the experienced memory is stored with the emotions still active (like putting a TV in the closet when it's still on). Later, when something causes the memory to be recalled, it enters the mind emotionally active instead of as wisdom. This emotional load from the past effectively adds the intensity of the past memory to the current event, thus throwing off the brain's judgment of how important the current event actually is. Have you ever met someone who perpetually had issues with men, women, or authority?

3. Emotions that have no "return to joy" training— When the brain is missing the proper training on staying in a good relationship while feeling sad, angry, afraid, ashamed, disgusted, or hopeless, any event that involves that unpleasant emotion will not reach a mutual mind state. Without mutual mind processing, the memory remains emotionally active and specific emotions become FAR too important. We may avoid, warn others about, or express a "no return to joy" emotion far more than needed—even to the point of depending on the unpleasant feeling to create motivation. My father did not have mutual mind abilities with anger so he spent his married life avoiding his wife's anger and warning others, "You do not want to see me get angry."

4. Fearful (insecure) attachment styles—The three fearful attachment styles, which we looked at previously, produce 1) too little amplification (I don't have feelings), 2) too much amplification (it is all about my feelings), or 3) intense amplification of anything that might be fear producing.

5. Impaired executive function—This pattern is the basis for most of this book. When the executive (relational) fast track in the brain is impaired, the slow track (verbal, problem solving) management system goes into an uncontrolled amplification of the problem.

A well-developed group identity reflects back who we are, what we care about, and what kinds of things upset us. A group identity reminds us who we want to be, even if it is a difficult day. The group members function as an extended mutual mind network. In a secure group identity, people will notice and attempt to correct the judgment and distortions in others, reminding us who we are and working to keep relationships intact and bigger than the problems. Keeping relationships bigger than problems will be the theme of the next chapter.

DISCUSSION QUESTIONS

1. Could you relate to Joseph's story? If so, how?

2. Can you think of a time when your relational brain circuits were off in the past week? What triggered them to go off? How did you get them back on?

3. Share a story of a time when you saw a leader use one of the four relational strategies (CAKE) to help a group recover from an upsetting situation.

4. When have you experienced *hesed* in your life? When have you seen someone putting it into action?

EXERCISES

1. Use curiosity during a conflict this week and record how it impacts the relational connection in the conversation. Be prepared to share your experience with others.

2. Take time to share appreciation with someone each day this week. Tell them what they did that you appreciate and how it made you feel.

3. Identify someone with whom you have a strained relationship. Is there an act of kindness you can do for them this week?

4. The next time you find yourself needing to confront someone about a problem, try using the envelope conversation technique and see what happens.

CHAPTER 8

Act Like Yourself

The heart of Christ within us

IT WAS 7 A.M. and my (Jim's) first client had just walked in the door. It took him an hour in L.A. traffic to get to my office, but he was diligent and determined. We had been working on learning to look for God moments and opening his heart to the Spirit's work, and that morning he came into the appointment very excited.

"Jesus wants you to know that He created people with lots of 'be like' stuff inside them," he said as he sat down on my black couch.

I was confused. I had images of bees swirling through my head. So I said, "That doesn't make any sense."

He smiled. "Jesus wants you to know that there is lots of stuff inside of people that's ready to be like someone else."

Scriptures came to mind. Paul wrote that we are complete in Christ.[1] We have the mind of Christ.[2] We have become the righteousness of God.[3] Christ lives in us who have been united with Him in His death and resurrection.[4] It made sense that the qualities of Christ have been born in us through the Holy Spirit. They are present but dormant, and ready to be seen and called out.

In time it occurred to me that "be like" is a great way to describe the mirror neurons in the brain's identity center. Mirror neurons can't look at themselves. Our identity center can only look at others and activate the neurons that reflect what they see. If I live with people who regularly demonstrate disgust around me, my mirror neurons will reflect that and I will learn to think of myself as someone who generates disgust. If I live with parents who take delight in who I am and demonstrate that delight regularly, I learn to see myself as someone who brings joy to others.

Suppose the image of Christ within us is found in the "be like" stuff God put there. Suppose it is waiting to be awakened. We'll never see it if it lies dormant. It has to be identified and developed. So here is the problem: when we grow our identity in the world, we become like every other "mutation" out there, instead of the person God made us to be. When this happens, reflections of the deformities and dysfunctions in our world mold who we are rather than the heart of Christ lying undisturbed within.

> RARE leaders are really good at seeing Jesus in others and waking up that part of a person's heart.

Our true identity is like a seed. The entire DNA is present for the plant to grow into the unique plant it is designed to be. But if that plant is to grow into its true self, it needs to be tended and maintained. If this is done well, the plant will grow into a mature version of exactly what it was designed to be. When the plant fails to get enough water or sun or proper soil, or when someone steps on the plant or damages it in some way, the process of maturing gets disrupted. The identity of the plant has not changed, but its ability to fulfill its potential will not be reached in the same way it would have if it had been allowed to mature.

The idea that there are "be like" neurons in our brain can help us understand what it means to act like ourselves. Everything we need to "be like" Christ is already inside those of us who belong to Him. Much of it is dormant and needs to be wakened.

RARE leaders excel at this. They are really good at seeing Jesus in others and waking up that part of the person's heart. Most of us simply see the dysfunction and shortcomings of others. We fail to see who they really are, to see them as God sees them. Until we do, we cannot help them act like themselves.

ED: "JUST A CRANKY OLD MAN"

I (Jim) had a chance to practice calling out the Christlike qualities in a man who was mixed-up about what it meant to act like himself. We'll call him Ed Barker.

Ed was the gardener at the church I attended for several years. He was known for both how well he tended to plants and how cranky he would be with anyone who set foot on the church grounds. People would comment that they did not want to stop by the church during the week in order to avoid his criticisms of where they parked, walked, or crossed his path.

I began teaching a class that Ed attended. In the process of discussing our true identities Ed announced that he was "just a cranky old man. And," he added, "I have been cranky all my life." Since the discussion was about Ephesians 2:10 and how we were redeemed in Christ to do the good works God has prepared ahead of time for us, I answered, "I thought you said you were a Christian? Being cranky would be what you do when you forget who you are." From there the discussion went forward to the group identity Christians have of being a blessing to everyone—even those who think they are our enemies.

Although Mr. Barker had studied for the ministry and been a Christian for over sixty years, this idea came as a surprise to him. As a result he began to look at the factors that fed his "cranky ways" and ask God for help and healing. Within a year he was greeting people with a smile. Now it was impossible to walk on the church grounds without finding Ed with a smile and hearing, "Blessings on you!" in a cheery voice.

Ed's transformation occurred without being held accountable to a supervisor to make sure he treated people better. His transformation occurred as the "be-like stuff" inside of him came to life and he learned to be like Christ. As he discovered his true identity in Christ, he learned that it was more satisfying to spread joy than to express his "crankiness." The results of learning to act like himself brought improved life for everyone around him.

"WHO ARE MY PEOPLE?"

Identity sounds like an individual reality, but the truth is your identity always comes from belonging to a group. To be a pastor, leader, parent, wife, or athlete is to see yourself as part of the group of people who bear that title. Your core identity flows out of your answer to the question, "Who are my people?" As Christians, we belong to a group called "saints."[5] We are children of God and citizens of the kingdom.[6] These are our people. Understanding which group we belong to helps us to remember who we are and how it is like us to act.

Taking my identity from my "kingdom" group also reminds me that I am not alone in this world. I belong to a larger community, thus, part of acting like myself is to think of their needs as well as my own. We express the highest version of ourselves when we live out of love. We deny our true selves when we think only of ourselves and not of our group as well. Therefore, Paul wrote,

> *Make my joy complete by being like-minded, having the same love, being one in spirit and of one mind. Do nothing out of selfish ambition or vain conceit. Rather, in humility value others above yourselves, not looking to your own interests but each of you to the interests of the others.*[7]

This is a good description of the type of group thinking that is to characterize Christians when we remember who we are, who our people are, and how it is like us to act. However, rather than living from our identity in Christ, all too often we define ourselves by our malfunctions and shortcomings. When we forget who we are, we need someone to remind us of how it is like our people to act.

PROTECTORS, POSSUMS, AND PREDATORS

When I as a Christian leader live out of that identity, I will always function as a protector for my group. To live any other way, would be a distortion of my true identity. The Bible describes three types of shepherd leaders:

- Good shepherds who protect the flock and lay down their lives for the sheep.[8]
- Hirelings, who run at the first sign of trouble because they do not care about the sheep and are only in it for the money.[9]
- Bad shepherds who devour the flock and use the sheep for their own self-indulgence and pleasure.[10]

The classic image of a protector leader in the Bible is the good shepherd. Sheep don't have to worry when the good shepherd is around. They don't have to worry that the shepherd will use them and abuse them. They know he is willing to put their good ahead of his own. Jesus accused the Pharisees of being bad shepherds who "devour widows' houses and for a show make lengthy prayers."[11] They did this to make themselves look stronger than they were and win the praise of men. Thus, Jesus exposed these religious leaders and labeled them 'hypocrites,' a Greek theater term for actors who went on stage wearing masks.

These three types of shepherds or leaders remind me (Marcus) of a scene in the movie *American Sniper* in which the hero (nicknamed "Legend") has a flashback to a time in his home when his dad talked to his two boys about who they were and how to act around bullies. The speech went something like this.

There are three types of people in this world. There are sheep, wolves, and sheepdogs. Now some people prefer to believe that evil doesn't exist in this world, and if it ever darkened their doorstep, they wouldn't know how to protect themselves. Those are the sheep. Then you've got predators, who use violence to prey on the weak. They're the wolves. Then there are those who have been blessed with the gift of aggression and an overpowering need to protect the flock. These men are the rare breed who live to confront the wolf. They are the sheepdogs.

This father trained his boys to see themselves as protectors who stand up against evil. This imagery helped the hero understand his role as a sniper. He was the sheepdog who kept the wolves (terrorists) from devouring the sheep (his unit). His identity as a "sheepdog" helped him know how it was like him to act when the pressure got intense.

PREDATORS

I (Jim) use a slightly different set of terminology to describe these three kinds of people. I call them predators, possums, and protectors. Predators (like wolves or bad shepherds) devour the weak. They have not learned to curb those predatory instincts that

> The essence of narcissistic leadership is its lack of tenderness toward weakness.

use weakness to their own advantage. Such predator leaders display clear signs of narcissism. Self-justified leaders don't know how to handle shame, so they deflect shame toward others. They justify themselves at the expense of others, and they pounce on weakness in order to grow their own power and indulge their own pleasure. In the book *Joy Starts Here*, I wrote about the subtle yet disastrous impact of a narcissistic leader.

> *Whenever groups who seek God fail to achieve a joyful identity, we can be sure there is uncorrected narcissism in the mix. It really does not matter who has the narcissism for the damage to be done. Narcissists deny faults in themselves and track faults in others. Narcissists justify their lack of tender responses to the weakness in others by pointing out these faults. "The way he answered me on the phone is not very Christlike and he is supposed to be the pastor," is just one of many ways to pounce on weakness. Where the acknowledgment of weakness would normally foster life and growth, predators punish weakness. Predators frequently scan the environment for signs of weakness that can be exploited for personal gain.* [12]

The essence of narcissistic leadership is its lack of tenderness toward weakness. Protectors who practice authenticity are tender toward their own weaknesses (by admitting them and asking for help), they stand up to narcissistic predators (as Jesus stood up to the Pharisees), and they draw out the potential in those who are weak. Their tender response to the weaknesses of others leads them to see value where others do not. It also motivates them to seek life-giving ways for those who have weaknesses to grow and contribute to the group.

Without training, we are all natural predators. If you leave a child to raise himself or herself, that child will not grow up to be a strong, protector leader. Quite the contrary, the child will grow up to be fierce and focused on doing whatever it takes to survive.

In a classic TED talk, Margaret Heffernan[13] tells the story about an experiment conducted by a Purdue University professor involving chickens. The concept was simple enough. He took two groups of chickens and counted the number of eggs they produced over six generations. One group he left alone to live life as normal. He did nothing to disrupt the breeding or the culture, and just let nature take its course. The other group was composed of what Margaret calls "super chickens." These were the top-performing chickens from each generation. The results were interesting, to say the least. The group that was left to themselves saw a dramatic increase in production over the six generations it was allowed to function. The group of top performers saw its production drop dramatically. In fact, only three of them survived. The rest were pecked to death by the others!

The experiment revealed that the so-called "super chickens" achieved their status as top performers by pecking at the other chickens and keeping their production low. She said, "The 'super chickens' elevated their production in comparison to the others by suppressing their output." In reality, these "super chickens" were more aptly named "predator chickens."

Predator chickens run a lot of organizations. They also find their way onto boards and into positions of influence in ministries and corporations around the world. Too many groups are starving for RARE leaders who will stand up to the predators in their midst and model authenticity. We need protectors who know how to live from the heart Jesus gave them and help others do the same.

POSSUMS

Possums (like sheep) are vulnerable people who tend to be hunted by predators. Possums only have one strategy in the face of danger. When

Possum leaders tend to disappear in times of crisis.

the going gets tough, they play dead. Without protectors in the environment, possums will never risk taking off their masks and being authentic. The risks are too great. However, if there are protector leaders willing to stand up to the predators, possums will feel free to begin exploring their true potential and begin contributing without fear.

Sometimes possums become leaders. They are often very nice people who like making everyone happy. The problem is that possum leaders tend to disappear in times of crisis. Overwhelmed emotionally by the magnitude of the problems they face, and relationally isolated, all too often they respond like the officer who stays in the foxhole during battle instead of remaining relationally engaged with his men and leading them.

PROTECTORS

Protectors are those who have a well-trained set of fast-track habits. Protector leaders are people with strong, joyful identities who welcome others and have tender hearts toward weakness. They do not exploit weakness but instead help vulnerable members of the group grow in joy. Protectors do not enable dysfunctional behavior but quickly protect the weak from it. When our group has high joy, its members tend to develop protector skills automatically. Since joy is the normal state of affairs, we naturally want everyone to share in the joy that comes from belonging to the group. We also naturally resist behavior that threatens our relational bond.

Treating weakness with tenderness isn't exactly a classic leadership theme. But every area of growth first appears in weakness and vulnerability. If we don't admit weakness, we can't grow. Beauty is often delicate and fragile, just as a flower is often the most vulnerable yet most beautiful part of a plant.

Joy levels build naturally around people who respond warmly to weakness. Anticipating a comforting response to our weakness lets us find help quickly. Problems do not get out of hand when weak people feel safe to seek help. This anticipation of joy creates adapt-ability. Without a validating response from someone who is happy to be with us, we will experience shame. When we fear being shamed for our weakness we hide our problems.[14]

Protector leaders are simply emotionally mature leaders. They keep relationships bigger than problems. They act like themselves without wearing masks so that people don't have to walk around them on egg-shells. They return to joy from upsetting emotions and help others do the same. They have the capacity to deal with hardships without getting overwhelmed to the point that they turn into a different person and stop remaining relational and acting like themselves.

In fact, protector leaders often don't realize they are unique. In their minds, they are just doing what any normal person would do. The skills they practice aren't done intentionally or as part of a strategy. Just like a great musician who has been thoroughly trained doesn't have to think about technique, and is free to play with emo-tion and passion, so leaders who have mastered protector skills don't have to think about what they are doing. It just flows out from years of practice. As a result, these valuable leaders often don't realize how rare their behavior is.

A protector leader will do such things as join in joy, share all dis-tress, and, this is especially important, encourage the weak to point out weaknesses in the strong—including the leader. How many lead-ers do you know who encourage that?

WHY WE STRUGGLE TO ACT LIKE OURSELVES

While there are many reasons why people struggle to act like them-selves, the two that deserve special attention are triggers and masks. We get triggered when our buttons are pushed and we turn into somebody we are not. We wear masks to make ourselves look stronger. Some of us have worn a mask for so long, we don't know where the mask stops and we start. In this chapter we are going to unpack both of these issues one at a time.

TRIGGERS

To understand how our emotions work, it may help to imagine that we each have a powder keg inside where we store up the pain and problems of the past. As long as no one disturbs the powder keg, we can function just fine. But when our buttons get pushed, it detonates something inside and our powder keg erupts. All that junk hidden just below the surface comes out and we turn into someone no one likes to be around.

Most of us deal with our buttons through avoidance. We craft a lifestyle and an approach to leadership that keeps people at a distance emotionally, so there is less chance of getting our buttons pushed. Avoiding upset emotions is not a recipe for success, however. At some point, we have to lift the lid and take a look inside the powder keg.

Recognize when you have been triggered. The first step to resolving any problem is to admit you have one. This starts by noticing when you get triggered. You know you have been triggered in several ways:

- You shut down relationally
- You blow up relationally
- You feel like running away
- You feel like punching something
- You overreact to the situation

In most cases, we aren't simply reacting to what has happened in the present. We bring all the stored-up emotions from past pain into the present.

Ask God what got triggered. As soon as you recognize that your buttons have been pushed it is a good practice to ask God if there was a memory that got triggered. In most cases, if you find yourself overcome by big negative emotions that make you act like someone you are not, it is because there is a memory or series of memories in which those emotions took root.

Ask God for a new perspective. Since God is always with us, He was present at every moment in our lives whether joyful, peaceful, or traumatic. He knows what we have experienced, the pain we feel, and what we believe because of our experiences. Taking the time to connect with God about the memories He brings to mind can give us a whole new outlook on their meaning and heal the pain.

Share what you learn with your identity partners. Isolation kills growth. It is important to share what you discover about your powder keg with other people. Telling others about your new perspectives helps to cement them in your brain. If you don't share such experiences with others, it can stay a left-brain event that doesn't have any transformative power. But when you share it with someone else, it becomes a relational event and impacts both the right and left sides of the brain. This makes it far more likely to stick as something that will change your attitudes and actions.

Seek additional help if necessary. There are times when all of us need help. Both of us (Jim and Marcus) have sought help from others in the process of dealing with memories and connecting with God. Talking to God and sharing with others will always be an important part of the process, but there are times when we need focused prayer with an experienced guide to get the breakthrough we need.

MICHAEL: "STOP CRYING!"

Michael is a Christian leader who used to take a very left-brained, analytic approach to life. There were several core memories that drove the way he lived. He recently explained how a painful memory from his past had contributed to an emotional problem in his present and how connecting with God changed everything.

> *I was born a very sensitive soul. My older brother was my hero and he was always bigger and tougher than me. I loved hanging out with him . . . playing sports and imaginary games. My dad was emotionally absent from me in my formative years and so my brother kind of filled a void in that arena for me. When I was*

eight years old we were playing outdoors and I somehow got my feelings hurt, as would happen fairly regularly, and I was crying.

On this occasion, he became very angry at me. I'll always remember that moment when he marched over to me and grabbed me by the shoulders and began to shake me rather violently. With rage in his eyes, he shouted at me, "Stop crying!" a number of times. Then he yelled, "You're a crybaby . . . I hate it when you cry!" I was so shocked and shamed. Being not only sensitive, but also very willful and athletic in my makeup, I vowed then and there that I would never cry again. And, I didn't for years afterward . . . not once. Then I repressed my memory of what I had vowed.

It wasn't until shortly after becoming a Jesus follower and a spiritual leader on my campus that I realized that something was amiss in my heart. I read in the Psalms how the great warrior-poet, King David, was able to weep as well as wage war. I prayed that God would help me to be more like him.

A few years later, after marrying my sweet wife, I opened my heart to her and told her about my inability to cry. Immanuel visited us in our living room that night and as we prayed while my head was in her lap, the fountains of the deep broke open and I wept buckets of tears. The Holy Spirit reminded me of the vow I had made at age eight and I asked the Lord to forgive me for hardening myself and to heal my wounded spirit that had been so ashamed.

I had allowed myself to get jerked by shame and the enemy's lie that "real men don't cry" into being someone God had never intended me to be. Nowadays, so many years later, if I don't shed some tears about something most any week I ask the Heavenly Father if I am hardening myself again somehow, since there are so many things in life worthy of our tears.

MASKS AND KILLING JOY

Masks we wear to hide our weaknesses and make us look strong to others are strategies we develop in order to solve problems. After a while, our masks become indispensable. They help us get what we want and avoid what we don't want. In *Joy Starts Here* I (Jim) explain it this way:

> By junior high we are cultivating a social image to win friends
> and influence people. [However,] our image management has a
> hidden side effect. Over time we become uncertain if people like
> us or our image. . . . Once we use our image to get results, dates,
> work, friends or avoid trouble and attack, the mask begins to de-
> velop a strength of its own. Masks that work make us dependent
> on the masks themselves. Since most masks make us look stronger
> than we are, we grow tired keeping up appearances. All masks
> slowly kill joy, even when they work.[15]

Most of us can relate to this description in one way or another.
We know what it is like to grow weary of keeping up appearances or
of wondering if people truly appreciate us or just what we can do for
them. Over time, not acting like ourselves solved some of our problems, but it created others.

HOW TO GROW THE HABIT OF ACTING LIKE YOURSELF

The three elements of a healthy regimen we presented in chapter 6 all
play a role in helping us grow in the ability to act like ourselves. Here
is a brief look at how I (Marcus) experienced my early journey.

Imitation exercises: praying like a lioness

I (Marcus) like watching how various people return to joy from upsetting emotions. Once I was invited to speak at a prison ministry breakfast in the Chicago area. A young African-American woman came up
to me afterward to ask for prayer for a relative who was in prison and
struggling with schizophrenia. It was clear she had been through a lot
of suffering in her life. While we were speaking, her phone rang. It was
her grown daughter. Her car had broken down on the side of a packed
Chicago highway. I watched as this woman entered into her daughter's
distress, validated her fears, and walked her through how to handle the
situation.

Without missing a beat she returned to our conversation. We all stopped to pray for her as she navigated these problems. Our prayers were pretty meek, but she prayed like a lioness. She thanked God for the trials. She thanked Him for the way He had always provided in every situation. She asked for the strength to be the warrior He wanted her to be. (She was calling out her own identity!) I learned by watching her. I got to see what faith under pressure looked like and see how to return to joy from upsetting emotions. My mirror neurons were watching and learning!

Paul set an example of Christian maturity in every church he founded. He demonstrated what it looked like to build a family and live as a community. Nearly all of his instructions have to do with how to live in unity and build a group that runs on love. In our individualized, Western way of looking at life, we have tended to take Paul's instructions almost entirely as rules for personal improvement rather than corporate engagement.

Having set an example for the communities he started, Paul often reminded them to imitate his way of life. This went far beyond his spiritual disciplines and personal holiness. It went to the way he did everything with the group in mind. Paul understood the power of imitation. We learn best how to act like ourselves by imitating the Christlike behavior in people around us.

Hearing God in a steakhouse

One of the first times I (Marcus) recognized that God was speaking to me, I was working at a Ryan's Steakhouse in Clive, Iowa. I was thirty-two years old with a wife and a baby girl. In the prior seven years I had served on the faculty of a Christian college where I taught Old Testament survey to college students and Hebrew to seminarians. Yet here I was waiting tables at a restaurant a long way from seminary. One of my coworkers asked me, "What are you doing here, man?" It was a fair question. I often asked myself the same thing. I remember saying something about needing to take care of my family during this season of life, but what I remember even more vividly was the clear, distinct thought in my head that said, "You are the only pastor most of these people will ever meet."

God was calling out my true identity. In a flash, I knew who I was and how it was like me to act in this situation. God was calling me to be a pastor to my coworkers. Almost immediately I began to recognize the open doors for ministry God was setting in front of me. My wife and I had several coworkers in our home for Thanksgiving dinner, and I often found myself in impromptu counseling sessions during coffee breaks. Being aware of God's voice helped me to act like myself in this situation.

Identity groups: reminding us who God made us to be

We all need people in our lives who know us well enough to recognize when we are starting to slip behind our masks and who can comfort us when we get triggered. Members of an identity group can say, "This isn't like you," or "It makes sense that this is bothering you because it is just like you to care about something like this."

Almost as clearly as I remember hearing God remind me that it was like me to be a pastor to those I was with, I remember sharing the experience with my group. That night, I came home and shared the experience with another couple with whom we shared a deep connection. Everyone was rejoicing that I had received such a wonderful insight from the Lord. Then my friend's wife said, "Marcus, God wants you to know that even if you were digging ditches, you would be a blessing to the people next to you." Her words helped me realize that my identity was not found in ministry (one of the lessons God was teaching me in that season of my life) but in being the person God had made me to be.

> "Even if you were digging ditches, you would be a blessing to the people next to you."

NO MORE HIDING!

One of the essential elements of redemption is the restoration of our ability to act like ourselves. Satan is the author of lies. He is the one who gets us to hide and pretend and deceive. He is the one who lies to us about who we are and what that means for the way we live. Christ came so that we might know the truth, and the truth might set us free.[16] Jesus came to restore what God had made us to be. Living out of that restored identity is the foundation of Christian leadership.

As a leader, when you learn to act like yourself, you create confidence in those around you. Fear gives way to joy and people don't have to walk around on eggshells when you enter the room. Such leaders don't try to hide their weaknesses, so people know they can trust them. And it is exhausting trying to be somebody you're not.

Brain Science for RARE Leadership

Slow track, fast track, and the "bullet train" of habits

Joy, identity, and mutual-mind states run in the brain's fast processor in the right brain at six cycles per second. Consciousness runs in a slow-track at five cycles per second. Many parts of the brain (on both sides) are involved with both tracks. The left brain is in charge of finding words, explanations, and sorting experience into processes we can understand. When the whole brain is working well together the different speeds of the two tracks allow us to remember who we are before we consciously think about the world around us.

Our relational identity is the fundamental interest of the fast track. When we know how to act like ourselves and maintain joyful relationships we almost never become aware that we have an executive running the show. The executive functions are so fast that conscious observations can never quite catch up. The fast track looks for joy and amplifies relationships and identity— who we are, what matters to us, and what motivates us even when life is hard.

Meanwhile, the slow track (conscious thought) amplifies problems as it sorts through our experiences. The slow track always focuses on problems just as the fast track always focuses on relationship. When the right-brain executive (relational) fast track in the brain is impaired, the slow-track (verbal, problem solving) left-brain assistant goes into an uncontrolled amplification of the problem.

Leadership involves developing a powerfully flexible and relational brain together with the ability to develop the same identity in our group. Leadership involves training skills and repatterning existing group responses. To understand repatterning better we should consider one more brain fact. Both the fast-track and slow-track systems are very flexible (therefore slow) gray matter. The brain has a "bullet train" that is up to two hundred times faster in the white matter. Unlike the gray matter that can change its response several times a second, white matter takes about a month to develop and is reserved for functions we repeat frequently but always do the same way. Are you thinking what we are thinking?

Any regimen we adopt for building fast-track skills needs to be done repetitively over a long period of time (more than a month and often for years) in order for white matter to build. When this happens, our brain will rapidly respond to all sorts of situations with the good patterns that have been trained into them. Without such training, our negative responses will always outpace our positive responses.

DISCUSSION QUESTIONS

1. How would you describe the difference between a protector, predator, and possum?

2. Have you ever worked for a protector leader? What characterized this person?

3. What masks have you been tempted to wear as a leader?

4. Have you been triggered in a way that kept you from acting like yourself in an important situation?

5. Have you ever helped someone else act like themselves in a way that brought them life? What was that like?

EXERCISES

1. *Imitation*: Practice identifying Christlike characteristics in other people and praising them for those qualities. As you notice people who have qualities you admire, begin to imitate them.

2. *Intimacy*: Practice appreciation for five minutes. Remember a memory from the past that brought you joy, or focus on something in your present that makes you happy, or think about something you are looking forward to. Notice how you feel as you dwell on these positive experiences. Give thanks for them. Give each one a title and write it in a journal. These are all great ways to jump-start the practice of appreciation.

3. *Identity group*: Share with someone (preferably your whole group) what you noticed this week as you do the first two exercises.

CHAPTER 9

Return to Joy

The "referee" within

IN COLOSSIANS 3:15, Paul writes, "Let the peace of Christ rule in your hearts." The Greek word translated as "rule" is probably better translated "referee." Now that creates an interesting image. "Let the peace of Christ be the referee in your hearts!" What would that look like? Well, what happens when a referee blows his whistle during a game? Everything stops until the referee sorts things out. In the same way, if I'm not experiencing peace, or the group I'm leading isn't experiencing peace, it's time to stop until we are all able to return to joy. Leaders and the groups they oversee all function better when peace is in charge than when upset emotions are running the show. In fact, the most important predictor of a group's emotional health is its ability to return to joy from upsetting emotions. The more often this happens, the stronger both the leader and the group become.

Sadly, too many leaders do not know how to let peace be the referee of the strong emotions within. As a result, strong negative emotions like anger, fear, and hopeless despair drive their decision making and sabotage their relationships. This chapter will offer several examples of what it looks like for leaders to return to joy from these emotions, and teach a simple model to guide you through the process.

FREEDOM AND MATURITY

To overcome the negative emotions that control us, we need both freedom and maturity. Freedom we find through forgiveness for deep wounds, tearing down strongholds, taking thoughts captive, and breaking ancestral bondage. One of the tools I (Marcus) recommend most often for this process is Neil T. Anderson's *Steps to Freedom in Christ.*

I had a friend who was very angry and mired in addictions. His marriage was on the rocks and he came to see me for help. Using the *Steps to Freedom* as a guide, we walked through his life story and uncovered a lot of deep pain in his childhood. That week we spent several hours processing his pain through prayer, forgiveness, and the eviction of unwanted spirits. The transformation could not have been more obvious. About a month later I was able to perform a ceremony in which he and his wife renewed their wedding vows. Soon, he became very active in reaching out to troubled teen boys. He became a father figure to them and a pillar in the church community. Experiencing freedom from his bondage made it possible for him to mature.

There is, however, a difference between freedom and maturity. To be set free from a compulsion is not the same as developing first the skill and then the habit of returning to joy from formerly controlling emotions. The man who found freedom in a week still had a long way to go in developing the habits of one who is emotionally mature. He understood that. Shortly after our time together he formed a 6 a.m. breakfast group with some other men in the church, and together they began a journey of growth.

About two years later, I got a call from this man's wife. He had died during the night of an apparent heart attack. As their pastor, I met with the family and helped with the funeral. The place was packed. All sorts of people—young, old, teens, and grandparents—stepped up to the microphone and told stories of how he had touched their lives in some way. God had transformed my friend, helping him find freedom and grow in maturity in a way that impacted everyone he met.

"Returning to joy" from upset emotions is a skill of the maturity my friend learned. How do we do this?

RETURNING TO JOY IS MORE THAN
ACCEPTING OUR EMOTIONS

The first step on the road back to joy is accepting that we *have* emotions. Emotions cause more problems when resisted than when they are accepted. Accepting our emotions provides much of the force behind Scazzero's *Emotionally Healthy Church*. We save huge amounts of energy when we accept emotions, which then allows us to calm ourselves quickly. Jim Martini, the CEO of Life Model Works, tells of his own experience of learning the importance and practice of accepting upset emotions.

> *I first worked with this [accepting emotions] years ago, after hearing that emotions were like riding a wave. If you let the wave break, there is a lot of intensity for a very short period of time, then you end up with a gentle ribbon of sea foam gently lapping against the shore. On the other hand, if you use all of your power to keep the wave from breaking, you become very tired and remain out at sea in the choppy, rolling water.*
>
> *I first tried this with anger. When something made me very angry, instead of stewing and trying to solve a problem or get in the face of the person that "made me mad," I rolled up a towel and twisted it while making my best angry face. Once the wave had crashed, I had the use of a sound mind once again to see if anything needed to be done to solve the situation that caused me to feel angry.*

Here Mr. Martini illustrates the skill of accepting emotions and calming himself. Learning to let himself experience the full emotion and deal with it directly allowed him to remain relational and act like himself, instead of dealing with people out of anger for several hours, days, or even weeks. Barbara Moon presents a simple way to learn to accept the six unpleasant feelings in her booklet, *Reframing Your Hurts*[1] for those who would like help learning the process.

Returning to joy goes a step further, because we now learn to respond well to others *during* the emotion and do not need to wait until after it is gone and we regain management control. In returning to joy we use the actual emotion to build a better relationship with others on the spot. Let us look at how returning to joy works with the six unpleasant emotions starting with how it would be to say, "I can sense and act like I value you as much when we are angry as when we are happy."

RETURNING TO JOY FROM ANGER:
"LET ME SEE IF I UNDERSTAND . . . "

Leaders are often angry! We get angry at incompetence. We get angry at blocked goals. We get angry with our coworkers, our customers, our bosses, and even ourselves. There is really no end to what can make us mad. When we don't know how to get back to joy from anger, we soon discover that it is hard to get anything done without this powerful emotion. We rely on it to motivate both ourselves and our people.

> I stopped listening to him about halfway through his rant and began planning my counterattack.

To return to joy from anger is not to get rid of anger, but to remain relational and act like myself even when I get angry. If I have this skill, I can still value you as much as when I am angry with you as I can when I am happy with you. As a parent, when anger is controlling me, I stop concerning myself with what is in the best interest of the child and get results through my emotions. It is the same as a pastor or manager. When I am controlled by anger, my relationship with you stops being the point and I just want to fix (or walk away from) the problem you're causing for me by making you understand how upset I am. I think or say things like, *What were you thinking? What's wrong with you? Do you have any idea how much trouble you're in?* And, *Get out of my office right now!*

Mature leaders (and parents) are able to quiet themselves and elevate the relationship above the problem. Instead of cutting off the relationship and using anger to get a desired outcome, I acknowledge my anger, continue to value the person, and address the problem in the context of the relationship.

When I (Marcus) was on staff at a church in the Chicago area, I found myself in a heated conversation with a good friend and co-worker. He was "lighting me up" and I felt falsely accused. The perceived injustice was making me so angry I could feel my ears get hot, my shoulders get tight, and the back of my neck stiffen. I stopped listening to him about halfway through his rant and started planning my counterattack. This was a clear sign that my relational circuits had shut down and that I had left the fast track in my brain and moved to slow-track problem solving.

It was about then I remembered the words another pastor had recently told me, "The next time you are tempted, stop and listen. There will be a still, small voice inside showing you the way of escape. Train yourself to listen for that voice." Here I was, my anger fully engaged, my heart racing and adrenaline flowing, when I remembered the advice to stop and listen. So internally I said a very spiritual prayer: "Okay, fine."

God knew what I meant. I was letting Him know I was open to suggestions on a different path than venting my anger. Immediately, a Bible reference came into my mind. It was James 1:20, which says that "human anger does not produce the righteousness that God desires." At first, I couldn't remember what that verse said. It actually distracted me from the argument I was having. Then I remembered. I had memorized that verse in fifth grade. It didn't take a rocket scientist to realize that God didn't want my anger to provide guidance, but I was already mad so I prayed mentally, "Could You be more specific?" (I'm not proud of it, but that's what happened!) God was gracious. Another reference came to mind. This one was Proverbs 15:1. It said, "A gentle answer turns away wrath." God actually gave me a more specific answer. This gentle answer would have been like me if I had been joyful with my friend.

By stopping to interact with God my relational circuits started to reengage. This allowed me to experience a "mutual mind state" (discussed earlier in this book) in which my thoughts and God's were able to get in sync with one another. The end result was that God helped me be relational with my friend. By offering a gentle answer instead of venting my anger, we were able to work through the situation and keep the relationship bigger than the problem. God made it clear to me that if my anger made me forget who I was, I would lose this relationship. My friend would forgive me, but he would never trust me again.

With my relational brain circuits back online and my mind in sync with God's, I said to my friend, "Let me see if I understand. You're saying there is a really big problem and that it is basically all my fault." My coworker took a step back as if someone had punched him. He stopped and said, "I guess it does sound like that. I think I'm just really frustrated and I am taking it all out on you. I'm sorry." With that we were able to restore our relationship and begin working on a solution to the problem together.

RETURNING TO JOY FROM FEAR:
"I CAN'T PREACH TOMORROW. WILL YOU PREACH FOR ME?"

Sometimes the challenge is facing a person you fear. Sometimes it is dealing with people while facing the threat of things falling apart. At other times it is facing a situation that triggers the fear of failure.

Kent is the senior associate pastor of a church in Orange County, California. Kent loves God and works hard at ministry, but lived with an underlying current of anxiety and depression. Several years ago, the Lord began working in his life to bring healing to some of the root issues of his fear and sadness.

Kent was introduced to the Life Model. Since then his life has been "radically affected by the concept of building joy and the rhythm of joy and shalom in our lives." A recent event illustrates how this training has helped him use the fear he once avoided to improve his relationships and return to joy. Kent says:

*Our senior pastor returned sick on a flight from Israel. I received
a phone call from him between 8 and 9 o'clock on a Saturday
night saying, "I can't preach tomorrow. Will you preach for me?"*

*In the past I would have stayed up half the night trying to
put something together and showed up in the pulpit stressed out
and in performance mode. This time it was different. Even on
the phone with the pastor I was able to quiet myself, listen with
compassion to him and ask the Lord what to do. I heard Him
tell me to say yes. I had a strong sense of His presence with me.*

Notice that Kent stayed relational both with God and with the
pastor. Normally, when fear gets triggered, people stop being concerned for others and think only of their own predicament. In this
case, Kent was able to maintain a sense of compassion for his colleague and how miserable it must have been to travel while sick. He
was also able to be relational with God and find comfort in His presence. The results of returning to joy instead of operating out of fear
changed the whole experience for Kent. Here is the rest of his story.

*I decided not to create an outline but to simply tell my story of
learning to practice interactive gratitude. It turned out to be the
most fun I've ever had preaching. There was a great response from
the congregation and momentum was set in motion to make
November a month of interactive gratitude. Because of what I
had learned over the last five years, I was able to stay true to
myself, be relaxed and authentic as I preached. It impacted our
senior pastor as well. He jumped right in and continued the
theme of interactive gratitude in his sermon series that month.*

"DAD, I KNOW YOU'RE SCARED"

My (Jim's) father lived to be over a hundred and spent the last ten
years with us. It wasn't easy; in the last few months we experienced
times of fear, hopeless despair, disgust, sadness, and shame. Fast-track
training in returning to joy helped me use all these emotions to build

better relationships. Some short vignettes can illustrate the simplicity of returning to joy.

Shame: Hospice nurses know they are helping families in hard times and arrive with as much cheer as they can. As I opened the door the nurse apologized for being three hours late and suddenly dissolved into tears. "Everything has gone wrong today. People angry at me, traffic . . . I'm sorry I'm crying," she said, digging in her bag.

"I'm glad we were the next stop on your list," I said, opening the door wide. "It must really be hard when people you try hard to help are not happy to be with you." (Shame is the opposite of joy so "not glad to be with you" is a way to say shame without causing a bad reaction if the listener is hiding emotions.) "Come on in. We have tissues right here." Just then she found her tissues and pulled out the package with a small smile.

"I know how much you try to be a help to the people you visit and I appreciate how carefully you take being a nurse when you treat my father." I went on to add a few details about her caregiving identity.

After that, this nurse always showed up at the door with a smile that shone like a new penny and lost her somewhat stiff edges—while giving excellent care.

Fear: My father struggled to breathe as the paramedics and the doctor came into the emergency room. Dad looked scared and the distorted rhythms I saw on the heart monitor added to my fear. Just then my spiritual daughter Eileen arrived, looking clearly frightened by the near-death scene in front of her. She took one of his hands and I the other. "Dad, I know you are scared. We all get scared when we cannot breathe. Eileen is here and we are glad you are not alone. She is going to read some of your favorite Psalms while we wait and see what the doctors can do."

> "It is good to have my brother here," I said to him.

It was being together in the very fear of the gasps, the missing heartbeats, and the beeping machines that brought us the joy that in such times we were not alone. As Eileen read the Scriptures, all three of us relaxed a bit, comforted by knowing who we were and *whose* we were at such times of fear.

Hopeless despair: "Nothing will help," I told my brother Tim as Dad became increasingly agitated in bed. Tim was with us to help for as long as his vacation time allowed. He knew the medications the hospice nurse had left, and I explained what happened with each choice. Tim finally looked at me with the recognition in his eyes that there was no hope of a simple solution.

"It is good to have my brother here," I said to him. It was quiet for a while except for thrashing from Dad. Sometimes saying less is more. I could have said what a good brother and son Tim was, but the words would not have improved the message. We knew that brothers stay together and care for parents, even when it feels hopeless.

Disgust: Our sons Rami and James each came for a weekend, taking care of Grandpa after he was unable to walk. This meant cleaning up messes. Occasionally Dad would take everything off and try to get out of bed, only to make a mess on everything. I taught them how to clean and care for Grandpa in the middle of the disgust that none of us could deny. Neither boy had experienced what it is like to really have your family need you before. Both commented afterward that they would have never volunteered on their own to take care of Grandpa but said it had been good for them.

Sadness: Dad had thrown everything off again and had his feet over the side of the bed rail. I felt a flush of anger at the mess. "What are you doing, Dad?"

"I'm going up to heaven!" he replied, struggling harder.

"No you are not, Dad," I said, feeling the rising sadness of this disappointing news.

"Where am I then?" he asked.

"You are in Pasadena, Dad." He stopped struggling and slumped back.

"Oh!" he said, "Pasadena. That is so second-rate."

"Here, let me cover you up and get your oxygen hooked up again." My actions let him know I was glad to be with him in this sad moment. It was the only moment when Dad and I actually shared how sad his decline had been to watch. Pasadena was indeed so second-rate. It was a moment of knowing who we were as father and son—both sons of a better Father and citizens of a better world. We found joy in the company of sadness, in effect saying, *I value you as much now as when we are happy.*

TURNING ON THE VCR

We've briefly mentioned this before. We must learn the skills of Validation, Comfort, and Repattern if we are to return to joy from unpleasant emotions. This is a "repeat after me" form of learning that repatterns the way our brain "speaks" to itself. We repattern as we speak aloud.

> To validate an emotion doesn't mean you have to agree with it.

The validation and comfort pattern helps us and others return to joy from upsetting emotions. Validation and comfort can be used in conversation but is essential in our self-talk. Let us learn to VCR.

Validate—To validate an emotion does not mean you have to agree with it. It means you are able to 1) name the emotion, 2) recognize where it originated, and 3) understand the level of intensity. If someone comes into my office angry about a situation, I may not agree that they have a rational reason to be angry. But I can still identify the emotion and meet them there.

"I see you are really angry that management has made a deduction from your pay (Validation). Why don't we see if we can straighten this out?" (Comfort)

Notice what a response like this does:

- It meets the person in *their* emotion (not yours)
- It names the emotion accurately
- It provides some sense that you understand why they feel the way they do (if you don't, then take the time to listen long enough to find out)

Validation makes people feel understood and greatly helps their fast-track elevator to move through the third floor (where emotions sync up) efficiently. Validation helps us synchronize with their emotions and meet them where they are. When people feel understood, they tend to be far more open to whatever explanation or correction you may have to offer.

If you skip the validation process and go straight to correction, you may win the argument and shut down the disagreement, but you will damage the relationship and feed the level of toxicity in the environment. Skipping validation is a classic blunder made by people who are used to problems being more important than relationships.

Validation is a skill we use with ourselves as well as with others. It is an important part of our self-talk. Validating ourselves is simply identifying the starting point from which we need to recover. For example:

"Yes, I'm kind of angry right now."

"You're feeling some shame about being corrected, aren't you?"

"Hearing of another fight between Steve and Lisa makes me and the rest of the church staff feel hopeless."

I (Marcus) once worked with a group of leaders at a large church who were dealing with the fallout of an affair on the staff (sadly, this is not an uncommon event). As we got started, we began with a validation exercise. I encouraged everyone in the group to share the dominant emotion they were feeling in the wake of this unexpected tragedy. Some said they were in shock; some were feeling deep grief; others were angry; still others felt betrayed. As we went around the room and shared, you could feel the tension draining away. They all shared that it felt good to know they weren't alone in feeling deep emotions. In not more than fifteen minutes, the entire atmosphere in the room had changed. As the leaders shared from their hearts, they felt more connected and more hopeful, and we hadn't even started problem solving yet.

Comfort—After the validation exercise, we turned to comforting. I started by offering a common paradigm about why such things tend to happen. I shared how communities often enter into unspoken contracts with their leaders in which they abdicate responsibility and transfer power to the leader, essentially making him their king. After all, *he* is the strong one. *He* hears from God better than they do. *He* understands the Bible better than they do. *He* has more training in ministry than they do, and God is obviously blessing *his* work. As more and more power gets transferred to the leader, relationships start to suffer. The leader becomes increasingly isolated because he has no peers. Soon, this very likable, gifted, and successful pastor starts playing the role of king. He answers to no one, and people start being afraid to challenge him on anything. This isolation sets the leader up for a fall. As he becomes increasingly alone with his burdens, the idea of an adoring, attractive female who just wants him to be happy becomes almost irresistible.

As I shared this perspective, you could see the light bulbs coming on all around the room, and people began sharing stories of how this was exactly what had happened. Offering a paradigm that explained the situation was comforting to them and made the problem feel more manageable. They immediately realized that their whole leadership culture had contributed to this problem and that very practical changes were going to need to be made.

Based on the work done in that meeting, this team of godly leaders was now ready to do the hard work of building new patterns in their leadership culture that would create a more open and emotionally healthy environment. They were beginning to recover.

The primary way we comfort ourselves and others is by providing a different perspective or alternative. In effect, comfort lets us know that however large the problem, our group identity is larger. There are still relationships and resources for us even when the problem cannot be changed. The temptation is to skip validation and go straight to this step. Most of us just want to fix the problem and make the emotions go away. We do this because we are not used to keeping relationships bigger than problems.

Repattern—Repatterning takes place when validating and comforting becomes the new pattern that guides our responses to painful or upsetting emotions. Returning to joy is not complete until we start operating out of this new pattern. If we don't learn to quiet ourselves through validation and comfort, our upset emotions will tend to grow as we fixate on our problems. If we are able to establish a habit of validating and comforting, a new pattern will develop that helps me return to joy quickly. As this happens my upset emotions will begin to calm and I will become more relational.

RARE leaders meet people where they are emotionally, find ways to help them change their perspective or fix their problems, and call out what is best in them. Leaders who do this build resilient groups who don't get stuck or overwhelmed by big problems or big emotions. Leaders who can't do this for themselves won't be able to do it for their groups. Instead of dealing with their group's emotions, they will avoid them or try to make them stop. Either way, they end up creating a toxic environment. Problems get bigger than relationships so people don't feel like being part of the group. When leaders stop acting like themselves, followers begin to walk around on eggshells, uncertain of what to expect or how bad their leader's reactions are going to be.

THE MOST IMPORTANT HABIT

Returning to joy may just be the most important habit you can develop as a leader. Leaders who return to joy do not lose their fast-track guidance or ability to develop the group identity simply because the leader or the group is feeling angry, sad, afraid, disgusted, ashamed, or hopeless right now. Right there in the presence of the feelings we learn how our group values our relationship, remains curious about each other, and protects others from being hurt. We validate accurately where the upset started and how large it has become. With both feet firmly planted on the reality of the situation and the importance of our relationships when things get this tough, we are able to quiet ourselves when upset individually and as a group. Learning to validate emotions before exploring how our group faces this kind of problem builds a strong sense of belonging.

The process of growing the return-to-joy skill (glad to be with you when one or both of us is upset) will almost certainly take you into areas of hurt in your past that have been stored up in your internal powder keg. Being intentional about dealing with these issues and involving others in your journey will bear fruit that is well worth the investment.

Jim Martini has read a lot of leadership books, been to lots of seminars, and run a leadership coaching business, so he has been introduced to some pretty high-end leadership training. Yet, if you ask him what has had the biggest impact on both his leadership and his life in the last twenty years, he would tell you that learning how to return to joy from each of the big six negative emotions is near the top of his list. Here is what he said in a recent email:

> *I still remember the day Jim Wilder told me that returning to joy is job one, the top priority. When he first told me this I started scheduling my prayer time for about 11 a.m. By that time most days, enough things would have gone wrong and increased my upset that I would definitely need some help returning to joy. Before he told me this, I might just keep gutting it out despite my upset for days on end. The problem was that I was no longer operating from a "sound mind" (2 Timothy 1:7) [KJV]. This was wearing on me, bad for those interacting with me, and might lead to either bad decisions or some serious withdrawals from the emotional bank accounts of those I was leading.*

RARE leaders think of returning to joy as the way to hit target #1 and build group identity. But when you think about it, how much of our lives is redirected by unhappy emotions? If we are making decisions to avoid fear, anger, shame, disgust, sadness, and hopeless despair, or sensing those feelings building in and around us, what kind of leader are we going to be?

DISCUSSION QUESTIONS

1. Which of the stories of returning to joy in this chapter were the most relevant to you? Could you relate to any of them? Which of the big six negative emotions (anger, fear, sadness, shame, disgust, and despair) is your biggest challenge?

2. Which of the big six negative emotions dominates your work environment?

3. Can you tell a story of a time you faced one of these emotions and were able to validate and comfort yourself so that you could remain relational and act like yourself?

4. When have you seen someone use validation in a really effective way?

5. Have you ever seen the VCR (validate, comfort, repattern) process in operation? What did it look like?

EXERCISES

1. *Validation:* Practice validating when you listen this week. When you find yourself in a conversation that elevates your emotions, intentionally listen for the emotions of others and validate their emotions before trying to make your own emotions understood. Observe what happens in the conversation.

2. *Intimacy.* When you notice an upsetting emotion that gets triggered, stop and ask Jesus if there is a root memory underneath that emotion and what He would like to show you about it. Write your thoughts on a piece of paper.

3. *Identity group*: Share with your group or an ally what you have written. Give them a chance to interact with you about your insights.

CHAPTER 10

Endure Hardship Well

Building our group capacity

NO ONE LIKES to suffer.

But suffering and unpleasant emotions can't be avoided. We all have to deal with them at some level. Those who learn to deal with them well become mature. They are a blessing to their families and their communities. Such people have a great deal of emotional capacity, which makes them very stable. It takes a lot to overwhelm them, which makes them very reliable. Their capacity to suffer well is one of the hallmarks that makes them RARE leaders.

No one likes to suffer. Even Jesus asked that the cup of suffering He had to face might be taken from Him. However, Jesus is the ultimate model of maturity in the face of suffering. Here are just a few ways He modeled, during His crucifixion, what it is like to suffer well.

- He remembered His mother's need and arranged for John to be family for her.
- He forgave those who were crucifying Him.
- He engaged relationally with the thief next to Him and played the role of redeemer for him (which was acting like Himself).
- He endured the taunts and mockery of His adversaries.
- He let Scripture remind Him how it was like Him to act.
- He remained relational with His Father throughout the pain.

We may be tempted to think, "*Of course* Jesus suffered well. He was the Son of God." Yet we see these characteristics throughout Scripture. Whether we recall Paul and Silas singing while in prison after an unjust beating, or we think through the "hall of faith" in Hebrews 11, it is clear that mature people handle suffering better than others.

THE SUFFERING OF A MISSIONARY KID

I (Jim) grew up in the Andes Mountains of Colombia during an era known as "*La Violencia.*" The conditions were similar to the massacres in Rwanda, as this was violence of neighbor upon neighbor. Mass murder and terror were daily facts of life for many. Estimates are that 250,000 people were butchered during the first ten years of my life throughout that mountainous region.

At two years old I suffered a stroke during a disease epidemic and a high fever that paralyzed half my body and led to a leg brace to keep from falling constantly. This significant deformity makes me walk with a limp to this day. As with most missionary kids of that era, I bounced around from homeschooling to boarding schools that included physical, emotional, and religious abuse. Missionary leaders who lacked the fast-track skills to keep relationships bigger than problems often resorted to punishments to manage children and "make good Christians" of them. From bullies to abusers, it all seemed "normal" at the time except for the most egregious violence.

One night at boarding school a mob with torches filled the road in front of us. We children huddled in the dark, looking out the window and praying silently. We all knew that a church near us had been burned down with everyone inside while the mob stood outside with torches and machetes. I knew I couldn't run with my leg, but my mind was on how to save my little brother. After an hour the mob moved down the road and we spent an uneasy night trying to get some sleep and stay awake at the same time.

My parents were very dedicated to their work, but both came from low-joy childhoods. My father had been in the local gangs before becoming a Christian and then a missionary. My mother had a significant brain defect that left her with virtually no sense of humor and a very low capacity for joy. This still did not stop her from touching the lives of over 2,000 women and children and earning their love. My parents had both faced severe hardships in their lives without much help in learning how to live with joy.

Today, when I teach on joy, some people get the idea that I think life should always be fun and happy. That's not what I mean. Joy is not a recipe for avoiding pain. Joy is what enables us to suffer well. Joy assures us that we are never alone in our pain and that those who share our suffering will show us how to remember who we are when things get hard.

CAPACITY: HOW MUCH STRESS CAN YOU HANDLE?

Emotional capacity refers to the amount of stress you can handle before things blow up or melt down. To understand emotional capacity it might help to think of a bridge. A covered bridge built in the 1800s to handle a horse and buggy will not have the same amount of capacity as a modern bridge designed to handle hundreds of cars and trucks. The beautiful, rustic wooden bridge simply wouldn't have the structural integrity to handle the weight of a semi-truck. In the same way, you wouldn't ask a baby to handle a task you might give your eight-year-old. Nor should you give an eight-year-old a job meant for a parent. When your emotional capacity gets overwhelmed, trauma occurs and your ability to suffer well gets stunted.

Emotional capacity is directly related to trauma. Trauma stunts the development of capacity. For example, if you want to traumatize a plant and stunt its growth, how would you do it? The simple answer is, "Don't water it." We've all

None of us had perfect upbringings in which we never lacked for anything good.

seen the effects on a plant of getting too little water. In the same way, the good stuff we withhold from our children traumatizes them. Their emotional growth gets stunted when they don't receive unconditional love or get enough hugs or receive the mentoring they need or a thousand other good things they often miss along the way. The point here is that you don't have to be abused to have some pretty big holes in your maturity development.

When you look at it this way, all of us are deformed at some level, because none of us had perfect upbringings in which we never lacked for anything good. This also means that all of us probably have some growing up to do in certain areas of life where that process got stunted during childhood. To borrow a phrase, we are all "unfinished" people.[1]

Many of the issues leaders face are directly related to the lack of emotional capacity they have developed because of unresolved trauma. When this happens, it is easy to get stuck in our maturity development so that we do not live with the level of maturity our position of responsibility and stage of life require.

FATHERS, MOTHERS, AND ELDERS

The Life Model was developed under my (Jim's) guidance by the team at Shepherd's House, a California-based counseling ministry. It talks about maturity in terms of infants, children, adults, parents, and elders. There is a natural course of development designed by God and built into the human experience. When all goes well, we progress naturally and happily from one stage of maturity to the next. However, when that process is disrupted by abuse or neglect things can "go sideways" in some pretty profound ways. Leaders who are stuck at the infant and child level of emotional development will find themselves frustrated and be a frustration to others.

The apostle Paul often referred to people as infants, young men, parents, or elders. In 1 Corinthians 4:15 he wrote, "Though you have countless guides in Christ, you do not have many fathers" (ESV). For years, I (Marcus) heard this taught as if it related to evangelism. Preachers said that there were no "fathers" in the sense that the Corinthians weren't fathering any children by leading people to Christ. There is some merit in that explanation, but it misses the bigger picture of what Paul was saying. The apostle Paul didn't just lead people to Christ and carve notches on his spiritual belt. He built a spiritual family. He was a father with many sons. He built relationships with these sons and mentored them as their spiritual father. Paul was telling the Corinthians that they lacked mature leaders who established significant relationships with their spiritual children.

The text contrasts "pedagogues" and fathers. A pedagogue was a slave who was assigned the job of teaching the children of a Roman aristocrat. Paul said the Corinthians had ten thousand of these teaching slaves, but they lacked "fathers." They lacked mature people who created "spiritual families" where young people felt a sense of belonging and learned what it meant to live out their new identity as a child of God.

Paul's solution to this was to send Timothy to the Corinthians. Timothy was Paul's "son" in the faith, and knew how to build and grow spiritual families. He would remind them of Paul's way of life in Christ Jesus. In other words, Timothy would be a model of maturity for the Corinthians to emulate. He would also help them build a multigenerational community in which weak and strong lived together.

The church today is in dire need of fathers, mothers, and elders—people with the life experience and walk with God to act like themselves, keep relationships bigger than problems, and model an intimate walk with God in the midst of hardship. Recently, I (Marcus) spoke at a gathering of women in Oklahoma City who took this model to heart. They referred to their leaders as mothers and matriarchs. Mothers "adopted" several young ladies and they did life together and spent time in mentoring relationships. Matriarchs built similar relationships with the "mothers." The result was a close-knit family with a strong sense of identity and belonging that was transforming people's lives.

THE FIVE LEVELS OF EMOTIONAL MATURITY[2]

Let's take a closer look at the five levels of emotional maturity taught by the Life Model.

Infant maturity—Infants don't know how to take care of themselves. But they are really good at letting you know they are upset.

They whimper and whine and wail in all sorts of ways and all types of circumstances. It is up to you to figure out what is wrong and take care of it. We expect this behavior from babies. They cry or fuss and we go through our mental checklist of what could be wrong: are they hungry, do they have a wet diaper, could they be teething, is it naptime? What isn't going to happen is any communication from the baby about what is wrong. You're not going to hear the baby say, "It's my diaper, Mom!" Or, "Man, this tooth hurts!" They can't tell you what's wrong, they just know how to make a fuss about it.

It is the same way with grown-ups who are stuck at infant-level maturity. You can be in your seventies and still have the emotional capacity and relational skills of an infant. Like the grandpa who grunts and jiggles his mug when his coffee runs out. He can't say the words, "Would someone please get me a refill?" He just makes his displeasure known. If he does speak, it is apt to be something like, "What's a guy got to do to get a refill around here!" The problem (an empty mug) is bigger than the relationships involved. The only thing that matters to him is that he is upset and no one is doing anything to fix the problem.

Infant-maturity leaders can be just like the old man with the empty coffee cup. The one thing they are really good at is expressing how upset they are. No one wants to get the boss agitated, and you never know what's going to do it. People around the infant leader have to learn to read him or her and anticipate their wishes because they aren't going to tell you what they need or how to fix any problems. They certainly aren't going to make treating you well a priority over whatever negative emotion they are feeling about their problems.

Child-level maturity—During childhood youngsters are supposed to learn how to take care of themselves. It is a time of expanding their skill sets and exploring the world around them. In this way they learn their place in the world (their identity), who their people are (belonging and identity), and how to act like themselves in a way that gets their needs met. A child is expected to be able to take care of one person—themselves. By the time they reach puberty, it is expected that barring a disability, they can feed themselves, clothe themselves, communicate their needs, and in general handle all of the responsibilities necessary to take care of that one person.

Children have the ability to tell you what is wrong. What they lack is the ability to take care of *you* and themselves at the same time. So, they usually default to taking care of themselves, whether you get taken care of or not. The person with child-level capacity is good at saying, "I need someone to get me some coffee. I need someone to make sure these papers get filed. I need people to take care of problems x, y, and z." What they are not terribly good at is remaining relational when they are problem solving.

The child-level leader is good at taking care of themselves and making sure they get what they want, but not so good at creating an environment where everyone's needs are getting met. The boss gets what he or she wants, or everyone pays the price.

For other child-level leaders the roles are reversed. While there is still only one person being cared for, it is the other person and self-care drops off the radar. In other words, whoever has the need gets the care at the expense of self, family, and everyone else involved. In stark contrast, there is never any question of how everyone's needs can be met when we work as a group.

Adult-level maturity—Adults know how to keep relationships bigger than problems, act like themselves in a group, and take care of the needs of two people at the same time. They have been practicing returning to joy from upset emotions for a while. Because of these skills, the adult is emotionally stable and relationally sophisticated enough to stay relational in the face of difficulty. You will rarely, if ever, see an adult turn to addictive behavior to cope with their stress.

Sandbox leaders always lack adult-level maturity. As a result they only know how to take care of themselves, and sometimes they can't even do that. They excel at letting you know they are unhappy. I (Marcus) am blessed to have a pastor (and friend) with strong adult-level skills. His name is Woody Cumbie and he is very good with people. I have watched him build teams and delegate authority in a way that has made for a strong and stable community. For several weeks, he met with me to do some leadership coaching (which is one of his other "hats"). This is where I really saw him shine. He did a great job of listening to me talk about what was going on in ministry and helping me focus my thinking on next steps in our discussions. I have gone to less mature leaders with problems and concerns and they usually end up saying, "Oh, I have a story like that," and the whole meeting ends up being about them. With a mature leader like Woody, I always know that he is going to remain relational and act like himself. He'll admit when he doesn't know something, and he has always been happy to meet me where I am, even when I have had to wrestle with some pretty big emotions.

> Most of our churches are not lacking for talented or gifted people. Yet they are starving for leaders with the maturity to love well.

Parent-level maturity—Once adults have practiced the RARE skills of remaining relational, acting like themselves, and returning to joy from difficult emotions for several years, they will likely feel ready for an even bigger challenge—parenting. Those with parent-level maturity are able to model and teach the skills needed to thrive in life to the next generation. This is what Paul said was missing from the Corinthian church. They didn't have anyone with parent-level spiritual or emotional maturity (which, in many ways, is the same thing).

They had a bunch of people running around the church looking out for themselves and complaining that their needs weren't getting met. But they didn't have a lot of mature people to guide folks into a deeper walk with Christ, a walk that expressed itself in love. There were lots of gifted people in the church (see 1 Corinthians 12), but not many practicing mature love (chapter 13).

Not much has changed, it would seem. Most of our churches are not lacking for talented or gifted people. Yet they are starving for leaders with the maturity to love well even in the face of the many problems any community will face.

Parents teach their children the fast-track skills they possess and help their children find additional resources when the parents have trouble keeping the family relationships more important than the problems of life.

Elder-level maturity—When parents have finished raising their own children, they are ready to take on the needs of the community. They begin to notice people in their group who don't have parents, or who at least don't have good parents. They will tend to take these people under their wing and include them as part of "their people." This gives those who need "re-parenting" a place to belong and someone to begin mentoring them in the skills they missed along the way.

Jim encountered elder maturity in South Sudan from a woman who took in young men who had grown up as child soldiers. She was re-parenting them and helping them learn who their people really were and how it was like them to act. I (Marcus) witnessed both my mother and my father doing this with hundreds of hurting people through the years. Around age sixty-five, my mother began mentoring young women. She would meet with them one day a week for ten weeks. During that time, she taught them their identity in Christ and took them through Neil Anderson's *Steps to Freedom in Christ*. Over a twenty-year period, she helped over 400 women process their baggage and build a foundation for a deeper walk with Christ. When she died at age eighty-five, many of these women showed up at her funeral to say thank you to someone who had done so much to help them.

The church needs elders. I don't mean people to fill the office of elder. I mean empty nesters who have raised their own families and have the life experience and relational skills to mentor a younger generation. Some of the most important work to be done in the church is waiting for our seasoned "life veterans" to step into the vacuum and make a difference.

GOLF AND MATURITY

I (Marcus) took up golf when I was a pastor. I was terrible. When I did hit the ball in the air (which was not often), it sliced wildly to the right. Some men in the church took pity on me and began to teach me how to swing a golf club properly. I often took my lunch break to go out in the field next to my office and practice hitting pitching wedges. I started to get better. One of my golfing mentors told me that I needed to swing a club 10,000 times before I would develop the type of muscle memory that made my swing "automatic." Since I lived in a cold-weather state (Indiana), he recommended that during the winter months I go into my garage and practice my swing for five minutes a day without actually hitting a ball. All of this practice has made a difference. I don't play enough golf to be really good, but I am at least capable of hitting some really good shots now and then. As with golf, so with maturity. It took a lot of swinging with a golf club to develop the capacity to play the game with confidence. In the same way, it will take a lot of practice to develop the capacity to suffer well.

But we have to practice the right things.

At a Dale Carnegie management class I attended several years ago I learned the expression, "Practice doesn't make perfect. Practice makes permanent." It made a lot of sense. Practicing the wrong swing in golf doesn't improve your game. Practicing bad technique in art or music or anything else in life won't help you get better. It will just make your bad habits harder to break. If we are going to build white matter in the brain that operates up to 200 times faster than our gray matter, it is important to make sure we build white matter around the habits of emotional maturity and not emotional immaturity. Here are a few suggestions:

Practice appreciation for fifteen minutes every day. Appreciation is simply dwelling on reasons for joy. Take five minutes three times a day and simply think about something that makes you happy. It could be a cup of coffee or your favorite food. It may be a special memory or something that is going on currently in your life. The more time you spend in a state of appreciation, the more your capacity for joy will grow.

This is sometimes not as easy as it seems. If you start doing this while you are in a highly agitated state, your negative thoughts can sabotage every attempt at appreciation in less than three seconds. I

(Marcus) was encouraged by Jim to develop this discipline. I remember trying to do my "appreciation exercises" at a time when I was experiencing panic attacks and living with a high level of emotional stress. I would hold a hot cup of coffee in a cool ceramic cup and try to focus on how it felt in my hands and how much I enjoyed the swirl of steam and happy aroma coming from it. As I tried to focus on appreciating this good thing I had, my brain attacked. Within two seconds, I would have sabotaging thoughts like, "This is stupid. How is a cup of coffee supposed to fix anything? Compared to the problems in my life, this is so insignificant. I should be trying to figure out a solution to my problems. [Expletive!] I'm such a loser. This is hopeless. I am never going to learn how to do this. What's the point?" With a few more expletives thrown into my thought life for good measure, my exercise in appreciation had turned into an exercise in hopeless despair.

This simply illustrates why it is so important to practice these things when you are *not* overwhelmed in order to build a foundation to which you can return. You have to build this capacity when you are not triggered if you want any hope of getting back there when you are triggered. In order to suffer well, you have to develop your capacity for appreciation.

Get your thoughts in sync with God's thoughts. Our ability to live at peace is directly related to our ability to be single-minded. When my thoughts are going in one direction, and God's are going in another, I am going to be double-minded and unstable emotionally.

One way to get your thoughts on the same page with God is to create a checklist of beliefs that feel true when your negative emotions are at their peak and begin to talk to God about them. I (Marcus) met with a former military officer who had become suicidal. I was visiting his church as a guest speaker, and some friends asked if I could spare a few hours to meet with him. One of the exercises we did was to have him pray and ask God to bring to his mind thoughts that were not in line with God's thinking. After praying, he began listing off the thoughts that came to his mind, without analyzing them too closely at first.

Most of his thoughts were about hopelessness, doom, inadequacy, and God's abandonment of him. I wrote them out and created a checklist out of the statements he had made. We then went through the list and talked about them one by one. I had him ask God about each statement, "Is this true? Yes or no?" Once he agreed that a belief was false, I had him ask God what the truth was that He wanted him to know. The next thought he would share was always something I could back up with Scripture as being true.

By the time he renounced and replaced the third lie on this list, he smiled for the first time. By the time we got through three more, he began to laugh. He was starting feel like himself again.

RECOGNIZE WHAT DRAINS YOUR JOY

What are the things that create low capacity for you? Part of being humble is recognizing our limits. The Bible never encourages us to hide our weaknesses. We learn to do that through fear of predators. Here are some common examples of things that can drain us:

- Physical issues: sickness, lack of sleep, lack of exercise, poor diet
- Relational issues: your spouse's attitude on the phone or before you leave the house, your children's lack of respect, a coworker's selfishness, office politics
- Unresolved problems: stress from financial pressures, fear of failure, anxiety about the future, conflict, huge expectations
- Recent loss: loss of dreams, of relationships, of possessions, of reputation

Recognizing that something has drained our joy means that we need to do something to reload. It can help to give yourself a break, do something creative, or get some exercise.

BUILD JOY BEFORE RELATIONAL ENCOUNTERS

When you know you are going to meet someone, it is a good practice to prepare yourself to make that encounter a joyful one. When I (Jim) would come home after a day of dealing with people's problems at the counseling center, I would regularly stop at the local park for a few minutes to set aside the concerns of the day and prepare myself mentally to be happy to see my wife when I walked in the door. I learned that being emotionally prepared to give her my undivided attention made a huge difference in our relationship.

AVOID JOY SUBSTITUTES

Capacity is like a bank balance. You can let it get too low. If your joy account is always low, you will constantly be bouncing emotional checks. You won't have the capacity to deal with the stressful situations life throws at you. When this happens we tend to turn to joy substitutes, better known as addictions. A person can be addicted to food, to alcohol, to drugs, to all sorts of experiences from sex to television. When my (Jim's) friend Ed Khouri was first learning to deal with the depression of living with constant pain, one of the joy substitutes he discovered was food. He found that he really liked muffins. Partway through the afternoon each day, he would reward himself for surviving his pain by announcing, "It's muffin time!" He would then enjoy this joy substitute to make himself feel better. The problem was that he began gaining weight and soon put on nearly sixty pounds.

> He would reward himself for surviving his pain by announcing, "It's muffin time!"

An encounter with Jesus began to transform Ed's inner world. He wrote:

> *Instead of feeling shame, hate, and fear about my weakness, I felt absolutely and totally accepted. My identity had been shaped by iniquity, fear, shame and the drive to perform. And now, at the weakest point of my entire life, Jesus told me that it was really OK to be weak. His presence in my weakness made me see that I did not have to try to be strong, hide weakness or perform, ever!*[3]

As Ed learned to find true relational joy, he also found that he no longer needed muffins to make him happy. Ed is one of the finest addiction recovery specialists I know. He will tell you from his own life and from the hundreds he has helped that without joy there is no lasting recovery from any addiction.

"AN INEXPRESSIBLE AND GLORIOUS JOY"

The key to enduring hardship is relational joy. This is a concept found throughout the New Testament as well as one that has been thoroughly confirmed by brain science research. Peter wrote that it was possible to be filled with an "inexpressible and glorious joy" in spite of enduring "grief in all kinds of trials."[4] James tells us to "count it all joy" when we "meet trials of various kinds."[5] It is not surprising that the apostles wrote like this. Jesus Himself taught the same things.

> *"Blessed are you when people insult you, persecute you and falsely say all kinds of evil against you because of me. Rejoice and be glad, because great is your reward in heaven."*[6]

> *"I have told you these things, so that in me you may have peace. In this world you will have trouble. But take heart! I have overcome the world."*[7]

Jesus also modeled victory through joy. We are told that Jesus endured the cross "for the joy set before him."[8] Notice how often the words "joy" and "rejoicing" are paired with suffering by Jesus and the apostles. This is no accident.

RARE leaders who have the capacity to endure hardship are not stoic, joyless robots. On the contrary, they are people who know how to enjoy life, and have spent years building joyful relationships and practicing ways of returning to joy from upset emotions. They are the sort of people you trust with your weakness because they know how to keep relationships bigger than problems and help people return to joy. You can be one of them.

DISCUSSION QUESTIONS

1. How does emotional maturity relate to the ability to suffer well?

2. Have you worked for a leader with adult, parent, or elder maturity? What marked them as different from other leaders you have known who were stuck at infant- or child-level maturity?

3. What drains your joy? Is there any way to make alterations to your lifestyle to address this?

4. Which joy substitutes tend to keep you from giving your time to what is truly satisfying and joy producing?

5. Did you recognize yourself in any of the descriptions in this chapter? If so, where?

EXERCISES

1. *Imitation:* Interview someone you have seen suffer well. Ask them to tell you stories of times they have faced hardship and how they handled it.

2. *Intimacy:* Talk to God about a hard situation or difficult person in your life. Ask Him to give you a new perspective on what is going on. Write down the thoughts that come to you. Pray for God to act in this situation and show you the part He wants you to play.

3. *Identity group:* After praying and writing down your thoughts, share those thoughts with the people in your group. How do they think it would be like you to feel about what is going on? How do they think it would be like you to act?

CHAPTER 11

Where Do You Go from Here?

Assessing maturity in yourself and your team

FOR EVERY LEADER who wants to improve, the next step is the most important one. The next step starts from where we are. This chapter helps us discover where we are. Both of us, Marcus and Jim, have a particular interest in having senior pastors, leaders of Christian organizations, and communities learn how to assess for missing elements in maturity development. Christians should be leading the way with mature relational skills and advanced EQ, but this is very evidently not the case.

Mature leadership is needed now more than ever. Terror, trafficking, and hate fill the airways. Imagine the difference in a church run by leaders who suffer well and help their people live with joy in the midst of hardship and a church run by leaders who measure success in terms of Sunday morning attendance. This is the difference between a RARE leader and a common leader.

I (Marcus) have a friend who fled revolution in his African country and now runs a ministry to refugees in the heart of Europe. This man lives with remarkable joy. I spent a week in his home and saw the life-giving way he leads his family and the priority he places on his walk with God and the relationships God sends his way. It is impossible to have a meeting with my friend without being greeted with a huge smile and genuine delight. Any conversation is certain to be filled with laughter and frequent words of appreciation.

Descended from African royalty, this man was born to privilege but now gives of himself in the name of Christ to people from all parts of the world, most of whom have never met a Christian. He tackles some of the most difficult situations a ministry can face—a constant shortage of funds and extreme needs of the very poor. Frightened people look to him for help with really big needs on a daily basis. If you tried to measure his success by the numbers, you might miss it. But he has succeeded in building a family and a community that regularly leads people to Christ, while spreading hope and joy to all who cross his path.

In stark contrast, many Christian organizations look good on the outside, but inwardly face no end of trouble. The numbers may look good, but the pastors are often depressed.[1] Meltdowns on the leadership team are often spectacular. Stress levels are high and relationships are strained. Instead of joy, our approach to leadership is producing tired visionaries, staff without emotional competence, and immature workers.

One of the primary reasons for such uninspiring results is that Western Christianity has been built to run on the weaker of our brain's two motivational engines. Instead of placing our primary focus on the stronger leadership engine found on the right side of the brain, we have been settling for getting work done with the weaker management engine on the left side of the brain. God has given us a powerful engine capable of providing the renewable energy source we all hope for, but it has often gone unrecognized and thus underutilized. The joy-fueled, fast-track processor on the right side of the brain has been hidden from view by the warped worldview of Western culture.[2] It has also been hidden by the sheer speed at which the right side of our brain operates. Our master processor is just enough faster than its counterpart to render its activity virtually invisible to the part of our brain devoted to conscious thought. Only recently has brain science even discovered its existence.

Recent studies of the brain have given us glasses to see past culture back to what the Scriptures have been telling us all along about the relationally competent leadership of good shepherds. The RARE leaders we try to emulate use this faster, more powerful engine; consequently they are less tired, less concerned about results, less fatigued, more joyful, more peaceful, and generally more admired, while producing people who are resilient even in hard times. The uncommon habits taught in this book can help you become a RARE leader who is able to stay the course without exhausting yourself and those around you.

FINDING NEXT STEPS

Assessments are very popular among leadership coaches. We assess everything from personality to intelligence. We commonly assess calling, giftedness, and passion. While all of these are good and have their place, we have found that nothing is more predictive of leadership effectiveness than personal maturity.

I (Marcus) have had a roller-coaster ride with leadership through the years. When I was young everyone told me I was a natural leader. I was elected president or captain of most of the groups I was in. I even remember one lady stopping me in the hallway at church when I was a teenager to tell me that she believed I would be the president of our denomination someday. It wasn't until I became a senior pastor that my real introduction to the world of leadership occurred. Before that, I think I believed all the press and figured leadership just came easily to me. Like a lot of pastors, I found leading a church both energizing and frustrating. When I was hired, my resume looked pretty impressive— two masters degrees, a doctorate, a three-year stint as a Bible professor, and staff experience at several large churches. On the outside, I looked like the ideal pastor. In some ways, maybe I thought I was. I was certainly trying to be. But there was no denying that I was frustrated, and that a lot of people at the church seemed to end up frustrated with me, too. There was something wrong and I couldn't put my finger on it.

> I was nowhere near ready to be an elder. In fact, I wasn't sure I was ready to be an adult.

My "aha" moment came when someone gave me a book by Jim Wilder called *The Life Model: Living from the Heart Jesus Gave You.* There was a chart in this book listing the characteristics of various levels of emotional maturity. It was the first time I had ever had a tool for assessing my own emotional maturity.

Suddenly everything made sense. I was in my early forties with a twelve-year-old daughter and a two-year-old son. I was clearly in the parenting stage of life, yet I was attempting to fill an elder-level role at the church. I was the senior pastor and head of the elder board—the functional "daddy" of the church family. On the outside, I looked like I could handle it. But on the inside, I was nowhere near ready to be an elder.

In fact, as I looked at the list of characteristics in the *Life Model* chart, I wasn't sure I was ready to be an adult! I had finally put my finger on the problem. A lack of emotional maturity was sabotaging my leadership potential. Before that experience, I had never even heard of assessing for emotional maturity. When it comes to leadership, it turns out that emotional maturity may just be the most important assessment we can make.

HOW EMOTIONAL IMMATURITY WAS KILLING MY MARRIAGE

The church wasn't the only part of my life impacted by this problem. My marriage looked a lot like my ministry. It had all the trappings of success on the outside, but inwardly there was something missing. I didn't realize it at the time, but my wife was dying emotionally. She tried to tell me, but I thought she was just overreacting. In my mind, I was doing the best I could. I scheduled date nights. I made sure I was home when she wanted me to be at home. But my wife knew she was getting the scraps, and it was killing her.

One night, when we were on one of our date nights, she opened up about it. "I feel like I am trapped in a cave with prison bars across the opening. You are standing outside like it's no big deal. You laugh and smile and talk to other people. Occasionally you remember that I'm there and you throw me some leftover scraps." She started to cry. I would like to say that I became very gentle and tender toward her and that I immediately saw the error of my ways and validated her emotions. But the truth is, I got mad. Why couldn't she appreciate how hard I was trying! We were on a date, weren't we? She was being unreasonable. Her expectations were unreasonable. She was just needy! That was it.

What I didn't understand was that my emotional immaturity was killing her. Just like it was sabotaging everything I did at the church.

Today, if you ask my wife, she will tell you that the best thing that ever happened to our marriage was the discovery of Jim's *Life Model* teaching. It is also the best leadership help I've ever received. I'm not saying my marriage is perfect and I'm still not a world-class leader, but I am much better at both than I used to be, and I feel like I am just getting started.

WHY ASSESSING EMOTIONAL MATURITY IS SO IMPORTANT

There are several reasons why learning to assess your own emotional maturity and that of the people around you is important.

1. **Assessments help you hire more mature leaders.** When we put emotionally immature people with great gifts, outstanding education, and genuine charisma in positions of great responsibility, we are setting everyone up for disaster. Things are not going to go well for that person, for their family, or for their organization.

2. **Assessments help to create a foundation for authenticity.** We all have areas of weakness. When everyone is honest about their areas of need, transparency becomes the norm and an environment for healing and maturing can be established. If it is simply expected that everyone has holes in their maturity development, we remove the shame from sharing what those holes are. We also avoid the idea that everyone has to be strong in order to be part of the group, or that if you aren't strong, you need to go somewhere to get fixed and come back when you are done.

3. **Assessments help us to know which skills we are missing or which need the most work.** This allows us to form a more specific strategy for personal growth and development. Rather than running everyone through a one-size-fits-all program, we can craft a regimen that is tailored to the specific areas of weakness we are trying to address.

4. **Assessments help us show tenderness toward weakness.**
Problem-focused leaders tend to use assessments to punish people for their weaknesses. Relationally focused leaders use assessments to learn how to help people grow.

5. **Assessments help us to be more effective in discipleship.**
Knowing where people are weak helps us to know where they need our protection and encouragement.

It is important to point out that we don't assess maturity in order to judge people or control them. We do it so that we can be as helpful as possible.

ASSESSING RARE HABITS

The four core qualities of emotional maturity can be used as a guide to assess your own maturity and also the maturity of the people you hire.

Remaining Relational

Keeping relationships bigger than problems is an important sign of emotional maturity.

1. Do you avoid conflict? Most of the people interviewed for this book mentioned that they are much more likely to confront people and problems now that they know they can remain relational through the process and return to joy afterward. When we lack these skills, avoidance looks pretty good.

2. Do you avoid people who upset you? I (Jim) know a senior pastor who had two doors in his office—a front door and a back door. If someone showed up he didn't want to see, his secretary was instructed to buzz him and tell them he wasn't in. It wouldn't be a lie, because as soon as he heard the buzzer, he would head out the back door and leave. Such avoidant behavior is characteristic of people who don't know how to remain relational when they are emotionally upset.

3. Do you use negative emotions (shame, anger, fear, disgust) to control people and outcomes? If so, you value problem solving over remaining relational.

4. When conflict arises do you make people choose sides or do you reach out to those who oppose you? Making people choose sides is a problem-solving move, not a relationship-building strategy.

Acting Like Yourself

We act like ourselves when we live out of the best version of who we are. If big emotions turn you into a different person, you struggle to act like yourself under pressure. If you have never developed a strong sense of your true heart, you may act like a possum or a predator instead of the protector God put it in your heart to be.

1. Do people walk on eggshells around you?
2. Do they feel safe disagreeing with you or do they keep their opinions to themselves?
3. Do they share their honest opinions regularly or do they wait to see which direction you want the discussion to go before they commit to a position?
4. Do people avoid bringing their problems to you?
5. Can they expect a tender response to their weaknesses, or do they fear any sign of weakness will be used against them?
6. Do you reveal your weaknesses and ask others for help?
7. Do you fear people discovering what you are really thinking or feeling about the problems you face?
8. Do you often present yourself as stronger than you really feel?

Returning to Joy

We return to joy by maintaining our capacity to be relational and act like ourselves during upset emotions instead of shutting down important parts of our personality.

1. Do you know how to quiet yourself when your emotions get upset?
2. Do you quiet well with others or do you isolate yourself during upsetting emotions?
3. Do you reestablish relational connection quickly after upset emotions, or do strong negative emotions control your relationships for entire days, weeks, or even months?

4. Do you help others return to authentic relationship quickly from their unpleasant emotions?

5. Do you see moments of upset as opportunities to strengthen relationships?

6. Do you stay annoyed with people who trigger your emotions?

7. Do you ignore people relationally when their emotions are not in sync with yours?

8. Do you help your group maintain an identity that is resilient in the face of difficulty?

Enduring Hardship Well

The key to enduring hardship is capacity. I may have a skill, but how developed is it? For example, I may be able to handle a certain amount of pressure and still act like myself and remain relational, but how much does it take before I get overwhelmed? We all have limits. Capacity is about expanding those limits so that we are able to demonstrate these skills consistently regardless of how our circumstances change.

In addition to the questions below, the maturity assessment charts in the next section can help you evaluate your emotional capacity.

1. How much stress does it take for you to avoid relationships?

2. How much pressure can you handle before you snap and turn into a different person?

3. How much can you handle before you disappear and turn to your cravings for comfort?

ASSESSING MATURITY

Several years ago, I (Jim) helped to develop a series of charts to help people do a self-assessment to see if they have developed the skills that are characteristic of each level of emotional maturity. You can use these charts to do your own assessment of where you may need some remedial work to live at the maturity level your age and life experience would dictate.

INFANT-LEVEL MATURITY ASSESSMENT[3]

Characteristic	Yes	Usually	At Times	No
I have experienced strong, loving, caring bonds with mother/a woman.				
I have experienced strong, loving, caring bonds with father/a man.				
Important needs were met until I learned to ask.				
Others took the lead and synchronized with me and my feelings first.				
Quiet together times helped me calm myself with people around.				
Important people have seen me through the "eyes of heaven."				
I can both receive and give life.				
I receive with joy and without guilt or shame.				

CHILD-LEVEL MATURITY ASSESSMENT

Characteristic	Yes	Usually	At Times	No
I can do things I don't feel like doing.				
I can do hard things (even if they cause me some pain).				
I can separate my feelings, my imagination, and reality in my relationships.				
I am comfortable with reasonable risks, attempts, and failures.				
I have received love I did not have to earn.				
I can give without needing to receive in return.				
I know how my family came to be the way it is— family history.				
I know how God's family came to be the way it is.				

ADULT-LEVEL MATURITY ASSESSMENT

Characteristic	Yes	Usually	At Times	No
I have had a rite of passage into adulthood shared by the community.				
I am comfortable in adult groups of my own gender.				
I have a peer group where I belong.				
I can partner with others.				
My relationships are marked by fairness and mutual satisfaction.				
I protect others from my power when necessary.				
I protect my personal and group identity when boundaries are violated.				
I live in a way that expresses my heart.				

PARENT-LEVEL MATURITY ASSESSMENT

Characteristic	Yes	Usually	At Times	No
I have brought others to life.				
I have an encouraging partner.				
I receive guidance from elders.				
I have peers who hold me accountable.				
I have a secure and orderly home and community.				
I can give without needing to receive in return.				
I see my family through the eyes of heaven.				
I include others in family activities.				

ELDER-LEVEL MATURITY ASSESSMENT

Characteristic	Yes	Usually	At Times	No
I have a community of people to call my own.				
I am recognized by my community.				
I have a proper place in the community structure.				
I am valued and defended by the community.				
I demonstrate hospitality.				
I give life to the "familyless."				
I help my community mature.				
I build and maintain the community identity.				

I (Marcus) have already shared about churches that confronted difficult situations with their leadership, such as the team I described in chapter 9 that needed validation of their emotions. The leadership team I met with was dealing with the fallout of having no means of evaluating emotional maturity in themselves or their pastor, and thus no strategy for meeting people in their weaknesses and helping them grow. The tool in this chapter allows us to begin a meaningful discussion about maturity in both existing and potential leaders.

"EVERY GOOD THING WE SHARE FOR THE SAKE OF CHRIST"

The average leader has not thought much about maturity and neither has the average organization that is seeking a leader or wondering what is going wrong with the ones they have. Maturity grows in a group, and we rarely consider the importance of our group's identity or capacity either as part of a leader's job or for the development of future leaders. The skills that create RARE leaders get lost as we focus on results and management as the primary target. Our cultural paradigms move our focus toward having better information and making better choices as the means for change. Spectacular failures by some of the best-informed leaders in the world have not caused us to change paradigms. We have seen that leadership is not the same as management but that many of us fall back to management when problems arise.

Leadership is about creating full engagement by our whole team with the important goals that need our attention. We have looked at how engagement grows out of our identity as individuals and as a group. When we are doing what we were born to do we will give our lives for the team and purpose at hand. Identity is powerful motivation that can be hijacked by fear to create really dangerous people. Identity can also be fueled by joy and transform the world.

Leadership is learned. In the center of a smoothly growing group lies the fast-track system in the brain of each participant that allows us to understand each other, think more like God thinks, and develop resilient character. The relational skills in this fast track have been called emotional intelligence (EQ), emotional competence, and relational ability. Learning, improving, and developing these fast-track skills is the basis for RARE leadership. RARE leaders remain relational, act like themselves, return to joy, and endure hardships well.

While many of us will need these RARE skills to save us from exhaustion and from dropping out of leadership altogether, the RARE habits are an invitation to go from good to great and become a RARE leader ourselves. This is the path that Paul offers Philemon when he says:

> I always thank my God as I remember you in my prayers, because I hear about your love for all his holy people and your faith in the Lord Jesus. I pray that your partnership with us in the faith may be effective in deepening your understanding of every good thing we share for the sake of Christ. Your love has given me great joy and encouragement, because you, brother, have refreshed the hearts of the Lord's people.[4]

DISCUSSION QUESTIONS/EXERCISES

1. How have you seen personal maturity issues affect your own leadership?

2. How have you seen personal maturity issues affect organizations you have served?

3. After taking the assessments in this chapter, where do you see yourself in the infant, child, adult, parent, elder model? Why?

   a. Which RARE habit is your strongest?

   b. Which RARE habit needs the most work?

Notes

Introduction

1. Travis Bradberry, "Emotional Intelligence," *Forbes*, January 9, 2009, accessed on November 3, 2015, http://www.forbes.com/sites/travisbradberry/2014/01/09/emotional-intelligence.

Chapter 1—Leadership at the Speed of Joy

1. See "The Fast Track System in the Brain" on p. 26.
2. See "Why We Ignore the Fast Track" on pp. 52–53.
3. See chapter 3, "The Elevator in Your Brain." See also "Breakthroughs In 'Seeing' the Brain" on pp. 63–65.
4. See chapter 9, "Return to Joy" and also the glossary on p. 212 for entries on low-joy capacity and low-joy environments.
5. Jack Ewing, "Volkswagen says Whistle-blower Pushed It to Admit Broader Cheating," *The New York Times*, International Business, November 8, 2015, http://www.nytimes.com/2015/11/09/business/international/volkswagen-says-whistle-blowers-pushed-it-to-admit-gas-car-cheating.html?_r=1.

Chapter 2—The Difference Between Good and Bad Leaders

1. Richard Davis, "We Need More Mature Leaders," *Harvard Business Review*, October 18, 2011, accessed June 4, 2015, https://hbr.org/2011/10/we-need-more-mature-leaders.
2. Stephen Covey, *The 8ᵗʰ Habit* (New York: Free Press e-book, 2005), 19–20.

Chapter 3 — The Elevator in Your Brain

1. Daniel Goleman, *Emotional Intelligence: Why It Can Matter More than IQ* (New York: Bantam Books, 1995; 2005), xv.
2. Allan Schore, *Affect Regulation and the Origin of the Self: The Neurobiology of Emotional Development* (Hove, UK: Psychology Press, 2012).
3. Allan Schore, PhD, Antonio Damasio, MD, and Karl Lehman, MD, have made major contributions to understanding the experience-processing pathway in the brain.
4. John 15:11.
5. Psalm 16:11.
6. Numbers 6:25.
7. Hebrews 12:2.
8. Matthew 5:12.
9. James 1:2.
10. Colossians 1:24.
11. Acts 16:25.
12. Nehemiah 8:10.

Chapter 5 — Don't Take Your Eye Off the Fast Track

1. See John Maxwell, *Equipping 101* (Nashville: Thomas Nelson, 2004), 14–18.
2. Jim Collins, "Good to Great," Fast Company, October 2001. http://www.jimcollins.com/article_topics/articles/good-to-great.html.

Chapter 6 — Where You Start: Imitation, Identity, Intimacy

1. John Maxwell, *Partners in Prayer* (Nashville: Thomas Nelson, 1996).
2. Bill Hybels, *Too Busy Not to Pray* (Downers Grove, IL: InterVarsity Press, 2009), 11–12.
3. E. James Wilder, Anna Kang, John Loppnow, and Sungshim Loppnow, *Joyful Journey* (East Peoria, IL: Life Model Works, 2015).
4. Psalm 100:1.
5. For more about building intimacy with God: *Joyful Journey* by Jim Wilder (with John and Sungshim Lippnow and Anna Kang) and *Toward A Deeper Walk* by Marcus Warner.
6. The VCR process is explained in more detail in chapter 9, "Return to Joy," under the section "Turning on the VCR" on pp. 168–71.

Chapter 7—Remain Relational

1. Jim Wilder and Ed Khouri have a list published online in 2009 called "Belonging Checklist for Relational Circuits" (Long Form Beta 2.0). www.thrivingrecovery.org/page32.php.

2. Derek Lovell, "Social Science Says Lasting Relationships Come Down To 2 Basic Traits," *The Mind Unleashed*, January 24, 2015, accessed May 2015, http://themindunleashed.org/2015/01/social-science-says-lasting-relationships-come-2-basic-traits.html.

3. 2 Timothy 3:2 ESV.

4. Paul McCabe, *Feed the Good Dog* (Ontario: Rose Line Publishing, 2004), 167, http://www.wow4u.com/wordsappreciation.

5. Steve Brunkhorst, http://www.wow4u.com/wordsappreciation.

6. Lovell, "Social Science."

7. Jeremiah 3:8.

Chapter 8—Act Like Yourself

1. Colossians 2:10.

2. 1 Corinthians 2:16.

3. 2 Corinthians 5:21.

4. Colossians 1:27; Ephesians 3:17.

5. The Greek word *hagios* ("saint" or "sanctified") and its variants is used over eighty times to describe those who are in Christ.

6. Galatians 3:26 (children of God); Philippians 3:20 (citizens of heaven).

7. Philippians 2:2–4.

8. John 10:11.

9. John 10:12–13.

10. Ezekiel 34:1–19.

11. Mark 12:40.

12. E. James Wilder, Edward M. Khouri, Chris M. Coursey, and Sheila D. Sutton, *Joy Starts Here* (East Peoria, IL: Shepherds House, 2013), 157.

13. Margaret Heffernan, "Why it's time to forget the pecking order at work" (TED talk, Monterey, CA, May 2015), https://www.ted.com/talks/margaret_heffernan_why_it_s_time_to_forget_the_pecking_order_at_work.

14. Wilder, Coursey, Khouri, Sutton, *Joy*, 16.

15. Ibid., 32.

16. John 8:32.

Chapter 9—Return to Joy

1. Barbara Moon, "Reframing Your Hurts: Why You Don't Have to Fear Emotional Pain," Joyful Musings, November 9, 2015, accessed November 10, 2015, https://barbaramoon.wordpress.com/2015/11/09/from-the-intro-to-re-framing-your-hurts-why-you-dont-have-to-fear-emotional-pain.

Chapter 10—Endure Hardship Well

1. John Eldredge, *The Way of the Wild Heart* (Nashville: Thomas Nelson, 2006). The cover states, "This book reaches out to 'unfinished men' trying to understand and live their role as men and fathers."
2. James G. Friesen, E. James Wilder, Anne M. Bierling, Rick Koepcke, and Maribeth Poole, *Living from the Heart Jesus Gave You: Fifteenth Anniversary Study Edition* (East Peoria, IL: Shepherd's House, 2013).
3. Wilder, Coursey, Khouri, and Sutton, *Joy,* 143.
4. 1 Peter 1:6–9.
5. James 1:2 esv.
6. Matthew 5:11–12.
7. John 16:33.
8. Hebrews 12:2.

Chapter 11—Where Do You Go from Here?

1. Dr. Richard Krejcir, "Statistics on Pastors," reported on a study done by *Francis A. Schaeffer Institute of Church Leadership Development* in 2007 estimating that 70% of pastors struggle with depression. http://www.intothyword.org/apps/articles/?articleid=36562.
2. The Enlightenment had a profound impact on all Western thought, including Christianity. One of the ways this is most clearly seen is in the voluntarist, rational philosophy that taught that good information led to good choices. Most Christian discipleship and leadership training has been built on this warped philosophical system. It has also blinded us to looking at different paradigms for life change.
3. E. James Wilder, "Maturity Stage Assessment" (2005) from http://www.lifemodel.org/download.php?type=assessment&rn=56.
4. Philemon 4–7.

Glossary

Here is a closer look at some of the terms and concepts discussed in Rare Leadership. *These definitions have been adapted from* Joy Starts Here, *which explores these and many more concepts in depth.*

Attachment: Attachment is the foundational connectedness and emotional bond that develops between people. Attachment starts with a mother-and-child relationship and characterizes all lasting ties between people.

Benevolent predator: This dominant predator is the "leader of the pack" who, it is hoped, will be a predator to outsiders, threats, or potential prey but protective to the group (tribe, pack, gang, country, troops, or corporation). However, when insiders become powerful they often are seen as threats and attacked or eliminated. Particularly attractive or vulnerable insiders are often preyed upon by these leaders. The vast majority of political, financial, military, sporting, union, corporate, social, and religious leaders fit the benevolent predator profile. "Revolutionaries and liberators" frequently start as benevolent predators, only to lose most of their benevolence once there is no external threat. Internal "threats" become the target, and their own people become the prey while the rhetoric blames some external enemy.

Bonds: Also known as attachments, bonds are the relational "glue" that holds identities and relationships together. There are two emotions upon which bonds form: fear and joy. Bonds are very specific attachments that do not allow substitutions to other people and become loaded with significance and meaning.

Fear bonds: A leading sign of abnormal development is relating to life and others out of fear. Fear is primarily the motivation to keep bad things from happening—we study so we won't get a bad grade, we go home so Mom won't get mad, we dress so we won't be embarrassed, we don't eat things so we won't gain weight, we exercise so we don't get fat, we hurry to work so we don't get fired, and we hide what we bought so Dad won't yell. These are all fear bonds and are quite common but all signs of a defective development of our identities, motivation, and brains.

Joy bonds: This desirable form of human motivation and attachment results from two people who are glad to be together. Not all joy bonds are beneficial, as in the desire to be together between two people who are each married to someone else. However, joy is the basis for all strong bonds and stable relationships. Being together is always of great value so joy bonds allow us to share both sorrows and joys.

Capacity: The neurological limit for being able to act like our relational self is a physical limitation on our ability to handle emotions and stress. Capacity is developed by training in joy, shalom, and returning to joy that is practiced with other people in a relational way. Exceeding our capacity results in a loss of synchronization in the brain so that our experience is no longer processed correctly, leading to the possibility of trauma and blocking the processing of traumatic memories. Our capacity can be increased by alternating strong joy and shalom experiences in our relationships.

Identity: From a brain science perspective, an identity is a complex and often confusing set of attachments and characteristics that define who we are. Identity is particularly difficult for humans because it is slowly established over time and always subject to changes from normal growth (now I am a mother), achievements (I am a driver), and accidents (I am a widower). Humans have aspects of themselves that are almost unchangeable (I am a girl), aspects that are currently being changed, aspects that are yet to be achieved (I am a great-grandfather), and aspects that are simply incorrect (I am worthless). By our adult years, the protection of our identity becomes more important than life itself. Let us consider some additional aspects of identity:

Group identity: While not well recognized in the Western world where independence is highly valued, we become part of a people as infants who are learning to relate and speak. During our young adult years, we form a peer-group identity that is further identified with our styles, values, and lifestyle. During young adult life, the brain is rewired so that the survival of our group becomes more important than our individual survival. We are also wired to think and feel many things in common with our group identity without being conscious of where this influence comes from.

Individual identity: We live with a mixture of true, untrue, and unknown aspects of who we really are. What we know about ourselves becomes our individual identity. All people have aspects of themselves that they do not like, and most of those are areas they consider to be weaknesses. The attitude they and their community have toward weaknesses will largely determine how much shalom and joy they will experience. God alone fully knows our identity, but God also uses kingdom people to help establish our true selves.

Joyful identity: While "joyful" is not an identity per se, identities will be motivated largely by either joy or fear. Most people's actions are predicted more accurately by what they fear than by what they say is important. Fear produces a low-joy environment. A joyful identity is one that is powered by joy and a relational style of interacting with other people. A joyful identity will retain resilience, creativity, productivity, and endurance more effectively than a fearful identity.

Joy: Joy is the twinkle in someone's eyes, the smile from deep inside, the gladness that makes lovers run toward each other, the smile of a baby, the feeling of sheer delight that grows stronger as people who love each other lock eyes, what God feels when He makes His face shine over us, and the leap in our hearts when we hear the voice of someone we have been missing for a long time. Joy is a relational experience that is amplified by right-hemisphere-to-right-hemisphere communication that is largely nonverbal except for voice tone. Joy is the life-giving feeling of mutual care.

Life Model: This is an idealized map for human development from conception to death developed at Shepherd's House Inc. in the 1990s. It formed the basis for many books and training programs. The Life Model is designed to be cross-cultural and based on Scripture and the best science, but without requiring a Western education to understand and use the model. The model was developed to explain how our identities as groups and individuals are restored.

Low-joy capacity: Our neurological capacity to regulate ourselves and behave as gentle protectors develops through practicing joy, and therefore we call it our "joy capacity." This capacity to withstand life is both internal and external, based on the neurological capacity we have acquired and the joy in our relational network. We have joy in both our individual and group identities, but when our attachments are weak and our life has been anxious, our capacity will be low and we will be easily traumatized or reduced to the fear and predator/prey responses associated with low joy.

Low-joy environment: Here is the place where people remember you (if at all) by what you have done wrong, what you cannot do, and by your weaknesses. There are many predatory interactions in a low-joy environment. Low-joy environments are places where the gentle protector brain skills are nearing extinction and the Immanuel presence of God is rarely noticed.

Maturity: We use this word in two ways. The first meaning is as a map for growing a full identity. We are mature when we have all the pieces well-developed. The second meaning measures our current development and says how we are doing for our stage of development. A mature apple blossom is mature for its stage but is clearly not a ripe apple. We can be very mature in one aspect of our identity and undeveloped in another.

Relational skills: The skills we are calling "gentle protector" skills are the links between our identities, relationships, and emotions. How we act (our identity) and interact with others to regulate, share, and quiet our emotions determines how our relationships will flow. People who learn good skills will amplify joy and shalom with others. Those who lack relational skills will amplify distress and make problems "larger."

Returning to joy: Restoring our desire and ability to be with others during an unpleasant emotion is the focus of these gentle and protective brain skills. The ability to care about relationships must be learned independently for the six negative emotions of anger, fear, sadness, disgust, shame, and hopelessness. The immediate result of "returning to joy" is a sense that we are not alone, and we then begin to quiet the distress. During the process of quieting we are still distressed and obviously not "joyful." However, quieting is much like the feeling of relief that comes from being found by someone who cares after we have fallen and cannot get up on our own. We might even give them a small smile. This is the return of joy during pain and does not look the same as joy by itself.

Shalom: When everything is harmonized and working together correctly—the right things are in the right place in the right amount so everything pleases God—we have reached shalom. In shalom all things work together for good for those who are synchronized with God.

Shame: Shame is not a single phenomenon but actually refers to two different emotions, one that derives from thoughts and one that is a response to others who fail to respond to us with joy. For the most part, the shame that comes from thoughts is based on lies about our identities. The other response we call *shame* is the reaction that makes us want to hang our heads and hide when someone looks at us with displeasure. The shame based on beliefs is predominantly left-hemispheric and is made worse if anyone agrees with it. Right-hemispheric shame is made better when someone shares the feeling with us and shows us how to stay in relationship while in the feeling.

Trauma: Trauma is damage caused by an impactful event that negatively alters our identity, integrity, or function. While trauma has traditionally been defined by the size of an event needed to damage an average person, we define trauma as the damage done when the impact of an event exceeds a person's capacity at that moment. Two types of events can exceed our capacity. The first is depriving us of something we need, and this always causes damage. The second type is events no one ever needs. These bad things that happen to us may or may not cause damage depending on our capacity at the time and resources immediately following the event.

Validation: Validation is a function of a secure bond that has been internalized by the three-way bond structure in the prefrontal cortex. Validation agrees with the person about just how big the emotion feels. Validation ensures that the relationship with others remains intact even if an emotion appears to be very large. Validation also perceives small feelings accurately without making a "big deal" out of them.

A Day in the Life of a RARE Leader

SHERRY STARTED HER DAY with a gratitude exercise. She made herself some coffee with a little cinnamon in it, got out her Bible and her journal, and settled into her favorite chair. After reading one of the Psalms, she began to write out her gratitude to God for one of His attributes. This led to about a fifteen-minute journaling experience that left her feeling connected to God as she began her day.

The day would be challenging, she thought. The nonprofit Sherry led was struggling financially. The board had been rather dysfunctional throughout its history. The founder of the organization had filled the board of directors with businessmen who were personal friends willing to donate to the cause and help him get his dream into motion. Most of them were more committed to the founder than they were to the cause. Since Sherry had taken the reins a few years before, there had been a lot of changes. Several board members rotated off. New board members were added. Policies were put in writing and meetings were run more quickly and efficiently. One of the policies that had been in place from the beginning of the ministry but never enforced was that board members would serve a maximum of two three-year terms.

Today, Sherry was having lunch with Bill, the founder's oldest friend and the ministry's biggest donor. Bill should have rotated off the board years ago, and Sherry intended to ask him to do so at lunch today. In a perfect world (from Sherry's perspective), Bill would step down but remain a friend of the ministry and continue to support them financially. This didn't seem very likely, however, as Sherry had discerned pretty quickly that Bill was a narcissist with strong predatory tendencies below his surface display of Christian activism. Sherry would need all of her RARE skills for this meeting.

Bill walked into the restaurant and started talking before Sherry could establish an agenda. "Sherry, so good to see you. It's always a pleasure to chat with you. Before we get started I just wanted to put my cards on the table and let you know that with all the changes taking place, I feel it is my duty to remain on the board and help you guide this ship according to the core values of our founder. I like your energy, but I believe it will give everyone a sense of continuity and confidence if I continue to serve."

Sherry's heart sank. She also felt a surge of nervous energy as she feared how this conversation would end. She also felt enough anger that she wanted to simply blurt out, "Fat chance, Bill. I don't think I can endure another three years of your posturing and manipulating." Instead, she took a more relational approach.

"I'm curious, Bill. Have you talked to your wife about this decision or any of the other board members?"

"Well, no. But I didn't think we were at that point yet. If you and I can settle this today, then we can bring them in on things. I'm sure they'll be fine with it."

Sherry felt a bit of disgust at his lack of consideration for his wife and colleagues. She thought, "Why am I not surprised?" However, she recovered from this emotion almost as quickly as it came and continued to remain relational. She decided to use an "envelope" approach by sandwiching her problem with Bill between two slices of relational bread.

"I appreciate your candor and realize how much you have invested into this organization in time, resources, vision, and emotional engagement. I definitely want to continue to have the best possible relationship as we move forward."

Bill stared at her. "You sound like you don't want me around anymore."

Typical Bill. Sherry was tempted to become defensive. She wanted to say something like, "Did you not hear a single word I said?" but again she opted for a more mature approach.

"Quite the opposite. I value our relationship and want it to be as strong and healthy as possible. This is what I am thinking. I believe it is important to establish a regular rotation on our board of directors. I am open to people returning to the board after a few years, but I believe our policy of keeping board participation set at two consecutive three-year terms is a good one. It allows us to continually develop a fresh group of leaders who believe in what we are doing and are willing to use their influence to advance the cause.

"I would like to propose that you consider filling a new role with the organization. As you know, the two foundations of any successful Christian ministry are prayer and finances. Prayer moves mountains, and finances pay salaries. We recently put together a prayer partner program to try to shore up that foundation. Would you be willing to consider being something of an ambassador for the ministry? You have a lot of influence with many of our partners. I'd like you to consider organizing two or three fundraising events in this upcoming year. This would help us tremendously, keep you in a vital relationship with the ministry, and allow us to uphold the new policy we have established related to term limits on the board."

"So you *are* trying to get rid of me!" Bill sounded almost triumphant. "Sam told me you didn't want me on the board anymore, but I couldn't believe it! You've only been with this organization for three years. I've been here for thirty! Who do you think you are, anyway! This is nothing more than a coup to take complete control of the organization for yourself! You're nothing but a narcissist after all, aren't you?"

Sherry knew that narcissists tend to attack when they don't get their way, but the force of his accusation took her breath away. Everything in her wanted to counterattack with equal animosity—

to put him in his place once and for all. After all, someone should have done this a long time ago! She felt totally justified in blowing up. Yet there was a still, small voice inside reminding her, "Act like yourself, Sherry. Don't let him control who you are."

Taking a deep breath and looking Bill straight in the eye, Sherry responded, "I'm curious, Bill, do you think your response is a good model of Christian maturity? Is this really the person you want to be? Or, is there a way for us to have this conversation without the personal attacks? We clearly don't see eye to eye on this, but *how* we get to a solution to our problem may just be more important than the solution itself."

"I know a power play when I see one," Bill retorted. With that he got up, made a show of gathering his things so that everyone could see him, and left the restaurant.

To say the least, things had not gone the way Sherry would have wanted them to go. She felt angry but also shaken, concerned about the fallout that would result from this conversation. She also felt a sense of shame at the way Bill had so publicly walked out on her.

But Sherry also felt an unexpected sense of peace. She had listened to the Spirit's guidance and handled the situation in a mature manner without resorting to all of the temptations of her flesh. "What now, Lord?" she prayed silently. She took a few deep breaths, apologized to the server for the scene that had been made, and ordered her lunch. She then called one of the allies from her identity group.

"Hi Alyssa. Thanks for praying. . . . No. He didn't handle it well, but I was able to keep my relational circuits on and stay connected with the Lord throughout the conversation. It was pretty stressful. I'm not sure how this will all end, but I really appreciate your friendship especially at a time like this."

Alyssa listened and validated Sherry's emotions. "So what are you feeling right now? If it was me, I'd be pretty nervous about what Bill is going to do next."

"Yeah, I'm definitely nervous. To be honest, I'm also a little disappointed with God. I was really hoping for a different outcome."

"So you're feeling sad and a little angry as well as having fear about where this is all heading. That's a lot of emotions and can't be easy to handle," Alyssa replied. "If I was in your shoes, I could certainly imagine feeling the same way."

Having validated Sherry's emotions, Alyssa attempted to comfort her by offering another perspective. "It has to get old dealing with difficult people. It's also frustrating to expect God to save the day and see things just get worse. Enduring hardship is never easy, but God clearly trusts you with this."

"Sometimes I wish He didn't trust me so much!"

"I know what you mean, but I can see you becoming a much stronger person than you used to be. I think God is growing your maturity, and I like what I am seeing. And you know, whatever happens, I'll be here for you."

They chatted for a few more minutes, then said good-bye. Talking with Alyssa helped Sherry return to joy and feel like herself again.

It is always harder to find peace when a situation is unresolved, but Sherry was growing in her personal maturity skills. She reflected on how she would have handled someone like Bill a few years before and said a quiet "thank You" to God for introducing her to the fast-track skills that had launched her on a new path—skills that helped her feel like herself regardless of life's circumstances.

About Life Model Works

LIFE MODEL WORKS is a nonprofit organization whose vision is to bring people into a thriving relationship with God, self, and others. Jim Wilder is the founder and chief theoretician of Life Model Works.

This book has introduced you to four habits that are integral to the Life Model. Life Model Works has a myriad of additional resources to train the fast track in you and in those you lead and influence. All of these additional opportunities can be found at www.lifemodelworks.org. A combined personal and community assessment is available at www.joystartshere.com.

The ideal fast-track training is THRIVE: www.lifemodelworks.org/thrivetraining.

Each spring Life Model Works invites all who are intrigued by our message to enjoy fellowship with like-minded leaders and compare notes on helping people develop a thriving relationship with God, self, and others. This Annual Gathering is also our annual opportunity to present our most recent applications of the Life Model. Look for it at www.lifemodelworks.org/events or subscribe to our newsletter to be notified of our next Annual Gathering: www.lifemodelworks.org/signup.

Life Model Works also offers regular webinars and a series of regional events: www.lifemodelworks.org/events.

Many of our books can be used as group studies, and our Connexus DVD series is designed to spread fast-track skills in your church or community: www.lifemodelworks.org/connexus.

The theory behind these fast-track skills is available in the THRIVE Lecture Series (search www.lifemodelworks.org/shop) and by listening to JIMTalks available by searching iTunes and other music download services for Dr. Jim Wilder or on disc from www .lifemodelworks.org.

If you would like someone from Life Model Works to speak at your church, group, or in your community please contact us at info@ lifemodelworks.org. If you would like to include fast-track skills inside a book or program you are developing, please reach us at info@ lifemodelworks.org.

About Deeper Walk International

MARCUS WARNER is the president of Deeper Walk International, a ministry devoted to heart-focused discipleship. The organization was founded in 1986 by Dr. Mark I. Bubeck, author of the Moody books *The Adversary* and *Overcoming the Adversary*. We provide training for counselors, pastors, missionaries, and lay leaders to help them be more effective in leading others to freedom and maturity in Christ.

The centerpiece of our ministry is **The Deeper Walk Institute**. It exists to equip life changers by providing high quality training in the various elements of heart-focused discipleship. The Institute consists of four courses: Foundations, Spiritual Warfare, Emotional Healing, and Advanced Issues.

Deeper Walk also offers training events tailored to the needs of specific churches and ministries to help them with issues related to leadership, discipleship, and recovery. For more about this ministry visit our website: www.DeeperWalkInternational.org.

About the Authors

JIM WILDER (PhD, Clinical Psychology, and MA, Theology, Fuller Theological Seminary) has been training leaders and counselors for over twenty-seven years on five continents. He is the author of nine books with a strong focus on maturity and relationship skills for leaders. His coauthored book *Living from the Heart Jesus Gave You* has sold over 100,000 copies in eleven languages. Wilder has published numerous articles and developed four sets of video and relational leadership training called THRIVE. He is currently executive director of Shepherd's House Inc., a nonprofit working at the intersection of brain science and theology, and founder of Life Model Works, which is building contagiously healthy Christian communities through equipping existing networks with the skills to thrive. Dr. Wilder has extensive clinical counseling experience and has served as a guest lecturer at Fuller Seminary, Biola, Talbot Seminary, Point Loma University, Montreat College, Tyndale Seminary, and elsewhere.

MARCUS WARNER (MDiv, ThM, and DMin, Trinity Evangelical Divinity School) is the president of Deeper Walk International. He is a former pastor and college professor who has written several books on topics ranging from how to study the Bible to spiritual warfare, emotional healing, and leadership. Marcus has done training events for organizations such as Navigators, Willow Creek Prison Ministry, and The Moody Church. He has traveled the world with Deeper Walk equipping people on the front lines of ministry with practical tools for dealing with root issues that keep people and ministries stuck and unable to go deeper into what God has for them.

Acknowledgments

I (MARCUS) would like to thank all of those who did interviews with me for this book. I'd also like to thank my brother Tim and my pastor Woody Cumbie for their help. I especially want to thank Jim Martini and Dawn Whitestone for their repeated efforts to help us express ourselves in a manner that would connect with a professional audience. I also want to thank the board of Deeper Walk International for giving me the time to work on this project and for their prayer and encouragement along the way. Last, but certainly not least, I want to thank my wife Brenda for putting up with all of the extra time away that went into this writing project and my daughter Stephanie who helped with editing and encouragement along the way.

I (JIM) want to thank my wife, Kitty Wilder, for proofreading and clarifying every sentence in the book. I also want to thank: Dr. Chris Shaw, Paulo da Siva, Rev. Chris Coursey, Dr. Bill and Maryellen St. Cyr, Coach Wayne Gordon, Kim Specker, Rev. Thomas Gerlach, Jim Martini, Gerry Petitmermet, Rev. Louis and Anna Kang, and Rev. Kent and Cathy Larson.

We both want to thank Duane Sherman and Betsey Newenhuyse for their extraordinary encouragement and insight throughout this process and for their exceptional diligence in seeing the project through to completion.

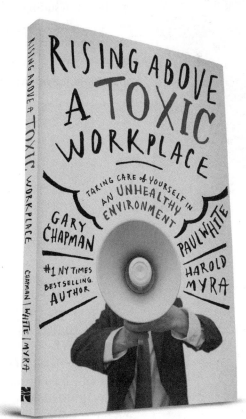

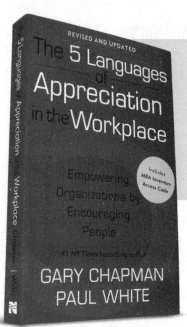

This book helps supervisors and managers effectively communicate appreciation and encouragement to their employees, resulting in higher levels of job satisfaction, healthier relationships between managers and employees, and decreased cases of burnout.

appreciationatwork.com

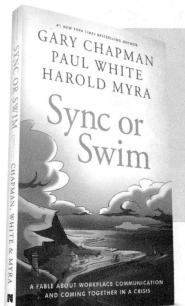

Sync or Swim is a small tale with enormous insight on ways you can empower, engage, and energize employees or volunteers facing discouragement or cynicism. Based on the principles successfully used by major corporations, health organizations, over 250 colleges and universities, government agencies, churches and non-profits.

appreciationatwork.com

Also available as an ebook

MOODY
Publishers™

From the Word to Life

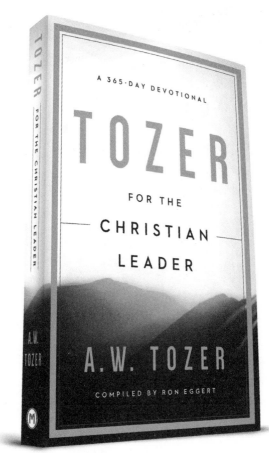

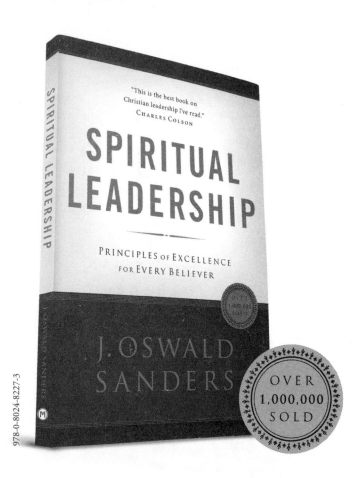

S anders presents and illustrates several magnifying principles
through the lives of prolific men. *Spiritual Leadership*
will encourage you to place your talents and powers at God's
disposal so you can become a leader used for His glory.

Also available as an ebook

MOODY
Publishers™

From the Word to Life

www.designyourdaybook.com

CLAIRE DIAZ-ORTIZ

DESIGN YOUR DAY

*be more productive, set better goals,
and live life on purpose*

978-0-8024-1294-2

WHEN IT COMES TO PRODUCTIVITY, hard work is half the battle. The first half—the crucial half—is planning well.

Enter the **DO LESS** method, a simple way to achieve your goals more often, in less time, and with greater peace of mind. Learn how to:

- Decide the right goals for you
- Create workable strategies for reaching them
- Harness time for maximum efficiency

Also available as an ebook

 moody collective

 MOODY Publishers™

MOODYCOLLECTIVE.COM